The Ecology of Stray Dogs

A pack of four urban street dogs. Larger breeds, as the German shepherds shown here, are seen roaming the streets with increasing frequency.

The Ecology of Stray Dogs

A Study of Free-Ranging Urban Animals

ALAN M. BECK

Chairman, Urban Ecology Task Force
Center for the Biology of Natural Systems
Washington University, St. Louis

YORK PRESS / BALTIMORE

363
B 38e

This book was manufactured in the United States of America.

Library of Congress Catalog Card Number 72-94644

ISBN 0-912752-02-5

Contents

FIGURES

TABLES

Preface

Dogs have been cherished companions to human beings since the dawn of civilization, and, in fact, probably for millenia before the advent of any civilized state. Accompanying the development of civilization over the centuries, ever-increasing numbers of regulations have come into existence to govern the conditions under which people are allowed to keep animals, particularly in urban centers. Some of these regulations have been concerned with the humane treatment of animals. Others have been directed toward preventing annoyance by animals or danger from them.

Whether or not they recognize a need for controls, most people find them objectionable, but usually they accept reasonable regulations without serious outcry. The various proposed or legalized restraints on pet dogs in cities, however, are often the subject of considerable debate and of quite intense feelings.

The emotional attachment of a human being for his dog is frequently as strong as the attachment that one human being has for another. We should not be surprised, then, when some dog owners react strongly against proposed dog control regulations in the belief, presumably, that the regulations are directed against dogs. Most such regulations actually are directed, instead, against people—the people who fail to meet their responsibilities in properly caring for their dogs and supervising them so that they do not create problems for the communities in which they live.

Most reasonable citizens, whether or not they are "dog lovers," recognize that stray dogs in cities do create real problems. Some are primarily esthetic problems, and these are important to those concerned with the quality of life in our cities. Others are primarily disease or safety problems, and these are of even more widespread—or at least more urgent—concern.

In this study many facets of the phenomenon of the urban free-roaming dog are examined. The focus is on one city—Baltimore, Maryland, the seventh largest city in the United States, and a city probably quite typical of large North American cities with respect to this problem.

This is a study both of dog ecology (and behavior) and of human ecology (and behavior). I hope that city officials throughout America and all humane citizens seeking insight into the problem of roaming dogs in urban America will find it interesting and useful.

Acknowledgments

I have often been complimented on the originality of choosing the urban dog as the subject for an ecological study. The truth is, the study was suggested by Dr. Edwin Gould, at The Johns Hopkins School of Hygiene and Public Health, who served as an advisor and who shared with me his ideas on methods, helped arrange funding, and worked with me in the field. His extensive knowledge of ecology and behavior, and his dedication to science, served as both guide and model.

To Dr. Charles H. Southwick, who not only served as ecological advisor and critically read all phases of the thesis which was the basis for the present book but who also gave so graciously of his time, I am truly grateful.

Dr. Miles Davis served as statistical advisor throughout the study and took time to read the thesis manuscript and to meet with me.

Mr. Edward C. Harmon, Jr., Superintendent of the Municipal Animal Shelter in Baltimore, gave generously of his time, made shelter records available, and permitted me to accompany his crews. Many thanks to him and the shelter staff.

The city veterinarian, Dr. David R. Berzon, willingly answered my questions and permitted me to review his data on the dog bite problem. His cooperation and interest are appreciated.

My brother, Gary B. Beck, and Anna T. Shaughnessy assisted with some of the field work, for which I am grateful.

Messrs. Charles Carroll, Sr., and Paul Morris of Baltimore's

Rat Eradication Program permitted me to join rat control crews on their rounds and shared with me their long experience with Baltimore's rat problem. The city's Department of Housing and Community Development permitted me to inspect vacant buildings.

I am indebted to Dr. Penelope Williamson and Mr. Sidney Brower of Baltimore's Planning Commission for letting me join their surveys of the city, and to Mr. Leonard Genova, Mrs. Patricia Morley, and Mrs. Audrey Rothschild who helped with interviews of residents of the study areas. Medical records and census data were made available through the kindness of Miss Lynn Bradley and Mrs. Dorothy O'Connell, respectively.

I benefited greatly from discussions with Dr. Richard G. Van Gelder and Alan Ternes (American Museum of Natural History in New York); Dr. Vagn F. Flyger (University of Maryland); Dr. L. David Mech (U.S. Department of Interior); Dr. Paul Heltne (Johns Hopkins University); Dr. Adrienne L. Zihlman (University of California, Santa Cruz); Dr. Robert B. Brander (U.S. Department of Agriculture); Dr. John Paul Scott (Bowling Green State University, Ohio); Dr. Michael W. Fox (Washington University); Dr. John F. Eisenberg and Dr. Devra Kleiman (National Zoological Park, Washington, D.C.); Dr. Joel E. Cohen (Harvard University); Dr. William R. Hanson (California State University); and Dr. Paul V. Lemkau (Johns Hopkins School of Hygiene and Public Health). To all of these my sincere thanks.

Financial and other help to support this research came from the Office of Vocational Rehabilitation of the New York State Department of Education (I am particularly grateful to Mr. William Eisner for administering my scholarship); the Society of Sigma Xi; The Theodore Roosevelt Memorial Fund (American Museum of Natural History); The Johns Hopkins University; and the National Institutes of Mental Health; as well as from my parents, Esther and Manny Beck, and from Marcia and Joseph Marymount and Susan Samuel.

My wife, Carol S. Beck, not only served as a most loving and supportive companion but critically read, corrected, and typed the first drafts of the manuscript. Special thanks to Gillian Emily Beck, who always welcomed me home after a long day in the field.

Introduction

Although there are good reasons to encourage ecological and behavioral studies of urban wildlife, such research is seriously lacking (Sinton 1970). Urban animals are pertinent to man for several reasons. For example, they serve as vectors of human disease and they provide insight into the effects of urbanization on man. Once their ecology is understood, urban dogs may serve as indicators of stress, pollution, and environmental deterioration, and as models for behavioral adaptations to urban life. They also may serve as epidemiological indicators, as Archibald and Kunitz (1971) showed with respect to sylvatic plague and Reif and Cohen (1970) with respect to pulmonary disease.

Hull (1963) lists 65 diseases transmitted from dogs to man. (The most common diseases from dogs reported in the Baltimore area will be discussed later, as will dog bites, which are rapidly becoming a major public health problem.) It has been hypothesized that early man lived in small dispersed groups insufficient to maintain many present-day human diseases. Measles, which is immunologically similar to distemper, may be the adaptation to man of the distemper virus; the role of the dog is widely recognized in the spread of rabies, especially as it occurs in South America (Bell 1967).

Flyger (1970) mentions that "Perhaps the primary reason for the study of dogs is the pervasiveness of dogs in the cultural context of all societies." *Canis familiaris* L. has been the companion of man for 10,000 to 12,000 years, and was possibly the first domesticated animal on earth. In the folklore of the Kato Indians of California, during the very creation of the world, the Creator "took along a dog" (Leach 1961). The remains of ancient hunting camps in Idaho show dogs—not tamed wolves—with hunter-gatherer man as early as 8,400 B.C. (Lawrence 1967). And fossils found in Missouri indicate that the practice of interring dogs was initiated by at least 5,500 B.C. (McMillan 1970), thousands of years before man came upon the idea of writing on clay. Obviously, man has had a close association with the dog since long before the dawn of history.

The dog probably was domesticated only from the wolf, *Canis lupus* L. (Borgoankar et al. 1968; Fox 1965; Iljin 1944; Mattew 1930; Scott 1954 and 1967), and much insight into wolf behavior may be gained from the study of dogs. Interestingly, the wild wolf has been studied more than the free-ranging city or suburban dog (e.g., Burkholder 1959; Crisler 1956; Jolicoeur 1959; Jordon, Shelton, and Allen 1967; Mech 1966 and 1968; Murie 1944; Rauch 1967).

In contrast to numerous studies of captive wolves and dogs, there are only a few field investigations dealing with feral dogs in rural areas (Nesbitt, in progress; Perry and Giles 1970; Scott 1971), and there is only one urban study (Beck 1971). On the other hand, there are more than a million laboratory studies using dogs (Flyger 1970) and many articles acknowledging the problem, the most complete being Carding's (1969) international review of stray populations.

Numerous articles have appeared in newspapers and magazines about the dog problem in cities and rural areas, and a few survey studies have been carried out (e.g. Kieran 1959; McKnight 1961 and 1964; Smith 1966). Information on the natural history of dogs derived from the present study apparently interests many people; it has been reported in almost every major newspaper in the country, though I made no public relations effort.

Man's influence on the dog amounts to having created

the species, with human selection and habitation being the main factors influencing the dog's evolutionary radiation. Furthermore, the dog probably affected human development. Scott and Fuller (1965) view the dog, domesticated about the time that humans started to develop group relationships, as a genetic pilot experiment for the human race. If domestication means evolving in a human-protected and human-controlled environment, then both dogs and human beings represent domesticated populations. Indeed, "urbanization and domestication have so much in common that it is not possible to define them as fundamentally distinct" (Parr 1966). The study of the dog might afford insight into human population dynamics (Scott 1954) in much the same way that Richter (1952) applied to man the physiological changes observed in the domestication of the rat.

Schaller and Lowther (1969) proposed that more insight into human social behavior could be deduced from the study of social carnivores than from non-human primates. They reasoned that since social systems are strongly influenced by ecological conditions, it is more important to consider a species' ecology than its phylogeny when choosing a model to be studied. They refer to carnivores of the plains and to early hominids, but their approach may be equally applicable to urban dogs and modern man. Southwick's (1972) studies on the effects of the urban environment on the aggressive behavior of rhesus monkeys may be another application of urban wildlife research.

Urban dwellers need some contact with nature for perspective (and sometimes even for sanity). For many this contact is their dog. City dwellers often place a high value on their dogs as companions and as protectors. The responsibly managed, well-cared-for pet certainly may have a place in city life; but allowing dogs to run free benefits neither dog nor man. A dog rummaging through garbage or quivering on the pavement after being hit by a car does not give the city dweller a sense of majestic wildlife. To quote McKnight (1961, p. 40), ". . . the dog is a domestic animal and in an exodomestic situation is at best pitiful, and at worst destructive and dangerous." The best interests of both dog and man dictate humane but strict control over free-ranging dog populations.

At this time, both dog and human populations continue to increase, and we can anticipate that dogs will go on playing a role in the lives of urban people. Their role will be very much a part of the ecology of man and dog, as they form part of the animate environment of our cities. If "Americans of all ages consistently demonstrate their craving to surround themselves with a bit of nature," as Tysen (1968) suggests, and if man really needs contact with a rich animate environment (Hutchinson 1971), then the value of urban wildlife study is well established.

Studying the readily available and approachable dog— a species that is large and mostly diurnal, is tolerant of human proximity, and in which individual animals are recognizable—can provide training for students of ecology and of behavior before they embark on research with wild canids. In addition, such studies should demonstrate to students in urban schools that wildlife study and research can be pursued within the confines of a major city. The present study was carried out entirely within Baltimore, the city with the seventh largest population in the United States, while the author was at The Johns Hopkins School of Hygiene and Public Health.

The Ecology of Stray Dogs

CHAPTER ONE

The Baltimore Study

The city of Baltimore where this study of free-ranging dogs was carried out is a port city, and the largest city in the state of Maryland. The 1970 census indicates a population of 905,759 people with approximately 53% being white, 46.4% black and 0.6% other races. The present population represents a loss of 33,265 (3.5%) people since the 1960 census, as well as a racial shift, for in 1960 the population was only 34.7% black (Census Notes 1971).

The city has 72 square miles of land surface, and about 12% open space. There are few large apartment-type houses. While the northern half of the city has many private houses, the southern half is known for its many blocks of connected row houses, numerous alley-ways, and narrow streets. The city averages 2.96 people/housing unit counting both occupied and unoccupied dwelling units with the density slightly higher in black areas, e.g. 3.37/unit in census tracts that are 90% or more black. There are 16,115 housing units (5.3% of the total) which are vacant year round (Census Notes 1971). Countless additional units are vacant for shorter periods, such as during construction and rehabilitation.

THE STUDY AREAS

Several different areas were chosen for study. Most of them are in the southern half of the city, where free-ranging dogs are most common. Each of the first three areas, which

1

were used for population surveys, is one-quarter square mile in size, perfectly square, and has a population that is at least 90% black according to census reports (Census Notes 1971).

The main study area includes the Reservoir Hill, Bolton Hill, and Upton areas of Baltimore and is just west of the Jones Falls Expressway, 3/10 of a mile south of Druid Hill Park. The white residents of the area are concentrated on a few streets running through the center of the area (Bolton Hill). This first area was the main focus of my study; it seems typical of much of south Baltimore with regard to housing type, population density and distribution, street topography, traffic patterns, and dog ownership.

The second area was the Windsor Hills section east of Leakin Park. Here there were a greater number of private houses than the first area. The Windsor Hills section was chosen at the request of the Windsor Hills Association, a neighborhood association concerned with local problems. The large number of free-ranging dogs was one of the problems that concerned members of the Association.

The third area in east Baltimore included the Johns Hopkins Medical Institutions complex. This area was chosen for its immediate access to the School of Hygiene and Public Health and also for its large numbers of dogs.

The fourth area was chosen because it contained a large dump which was used extensively by dogs. Systematic population surveys were not conducted here, but the residents who surround the dump and those directly across the street were interviewed. In addition, dog behavior at the dump was observed. This area is just northwest of Park Circle and south of Druid Hill Park.

The fifth area was on the grounds of an abandoned Paulist Fathers College (St. Peters) surrounded by woods at Chapel Gate Road and Frederick Avenue in southwest Baltimore. This area was chosen because of the free-ranging dogs that live in the woods and use the college grounds.

At one time or another during the study the entire city was visited for subjective impressions of dog activity.

FIELD METHODS

Whereas the dog population of Baltimore City includes all the dogs within the city's limits, this study concentrated on the free-ranging dogs. Reference to other subgroupings (owned dogs that are never on the streets and dogs in various kennel situations) are made only when related to the free-ranging population.

A free-ranging dog is defined throughout the study as any dog observed without immediate human supervision on public property or on private property with immediate unrestrained access to public property, as in the case of open porches, steps, lawns and yards without fencing. There was no attempt to distinguish owned and ownerless free-ranging strays, since licensing and collaring is so sporadic and the behaviors are so similar that separating the two categories is not readily possible or even necessary. Dogs not truly owned by one person or family were sometimes fed and protected by individuals in an area.

All field work during this study was on foot, or by automobile or city vehicle. I carried a 35 mm camera with a 105 mm lens, thermometer, and a small cassette-type recorder for recording behaviors and locations. I consciously dressed in neat work clothes so as not to call undue attention to myself by appearing as a city official. On different occasions I was asked if I was a sanitation inspector, dog catcher, newspaper photographer, or narcotics police officer. When using an automobile I placed magnetic signs on each side door which read "Johns Hopkins Univ. Dog Population Study." This lessened the suspicions of local residents and police. Once I became known in an area, residents would freely discuss the dog situation with me, and they proved to be a valuable source of information. Specific methods for the ecological parameters are discussed in the appendix.

CHAPTER TWO

The Ecology of Free-Ranging Dogs

ORIGIN

Free-ranging dogs were found to come from the following sources, which are listed in approximately the order of importance.

Pet Releases. It is a common observation in the early morning and evening to see a doorway open and a dog enter the free-ranging population. Interviews in the main area revealed that at least 37% of those who owned dogs permitted their pets freedom on the streets. Baltimore's row houses that are divided into first and second floor apartments give residents on both stories direct access to the streets. There are very few highrise buildings in the survey area and many of these are for the elderly and the occupants are not permitted to own dogs.

Pet Escapes. I never saw fencing more than 4 feet high in the lower half of the city; I observed dogs jumping over fences and climbing under them on occasions. Often a fence door is left open or is in disrepair, allowing pets to wander the alleys.

Breeding. The activities of a busy city do not usually interfere with mating behavior. Dog mounting and "lock" was observed in alleys, sidewalks, and streets, and amidst traffic and other dogs.

I followed the progress of one litter born under porch steps to a female that lived independent of man except for being permitted to use the area. The feral dogs in the Chapel

Gate area successfully raised pups of at least two litters in 1971, according to local residents.

Mating was observed throughout the year with a slightly noticeable increase in March. There is indirect evidence for breeding seasons. The Animal Shelter received an increased number of phone calls regarding free-ranging dogs on the streets during October in 1968 and 1969 and during March in 1970 and 1971 (see Fig. 1). The Superintendent of the Animal Shelter noted that people tend to phone in about strays most commonly when the dogs are observed in groups. Thus these peaks may indicate an increase of pack formation, possibly indicating an increase of breeding activity. There is a slight increase in the calls for unwanted dogs within two months after October and a definite increase two months after March (Fig. 1). Whereas this latter peak may be related to summer, it is tempting to hypothesize a spring and fall breeding season, or at least an increase in reproductive activity during these periods. This is consistent with wild canine breeding activity, though Engle (1946) had evidence that dogs have no breeding season.

Interviews have given me the impression that breeding is common but I have no real estimate as to its significance as a source of free-ranging dogs compared with pet release and escape.

Pets Abandoned after People Move. This source of free-ranging dogs was reported to me several times during my interviews and I once accompanied dog pound personnel to rescue a woman who was being terrorized by a vicious dog tied and left in a yard after her tenant moved from the area. People may abandon dogs because they do not know of the city's service to accept unwanted dogs, or because they distrust the dog pound due to the usual unfavorable reputation of all animal shelters.

Pets Released or Escaped after Having Been Stolen. This source of free-ranging dogs, too, was suggested during inter-

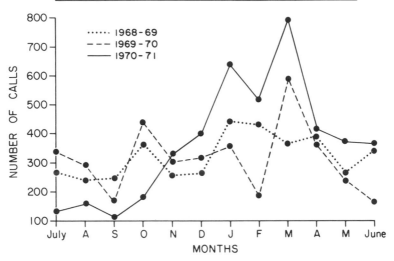

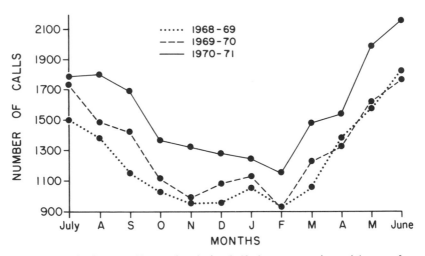

Fig. 1. Telephone calls to the Animal Shelter requesting pick up of stray dogs from the streets (*top*) and unwanted dogs from homes (*bottom*). Monthly totals are plotted for three years.

views, but I was unable to gather any statistics indicating its frequency.

ABUNDANCE

The free-ranging dog population was estimated by applying one or more of several different methods used to estimate wildlife to three selected areas of the city. (For technical details, see Appendix.) All of these methods of estimating the canine population were employed in the main study area. Throughout the study the dogs were "captured" photographically instead of by trapping. A summary of results for the main study area follows:

Schnabel's Multiple Recapture Method. After nine daily surveys, 170 dogs were captured (i.e., photographed), 34 were recaptured individuals, and there was a total of 65 recaptures. (Many dogs were photographed several times.) This method gave an estimate of 149 dogs for the quarter mile sampled, or 600 dogs per square mile, in 1970. (The probability is 0.95 that the true number of animals per square mile in the area studied is between 450 and 750.)

Darroch's Multiple Recapture Census Method. Of the 170 dogs captured as before, 107 were different individuals. Using this parameter, the population was estimated to be 612 dogs per square mile in 1970.

Hanson's Estimator for Unidentified Individuals. In 1970, after 14 consecutive daily surveys, I observed a total of 94 dogs in 59 groups, giving a group mean size of 1.59 dogs. Applying Hanson's (1968) formula to individuals, I estimated that there were 800 dogs per square mile. Using the numbers of groups removed (instead of individuals), I estimated 130.15 groups per quarter square mile, which when multiplied by the mean group size equals 207 dogs, or 828 dogs per square mile, thus comparing very closely with the individual removal method. This indicated that the model probably was not affected by the gregariousness of the animals.

In 1971, the individual removal and group removal methods yielded 635 and 628 dogs per square mile, respectively, after I surveyed the same area at the same time of year. This shows a loss of some 200 dogs from 1970 to 1971, but Student's t-test comparing the means of the numbers of dogs observed in 1970 and 1971 (183 in 262 groups, mean = 19.7 per day, and 205 in 283 groups, mean = 18.7 per day, respectively, for runs with comparable weather) does not indicate a significant change in the population of the study area. There have been no major social changes (e.g., no new laws) during the time in question.

Hanson's (1967) mean-variance estimator was also employed, but proved invalid.

In the Windsor Hills study area, which contains more private houses than the main site, proportion estimators yielded low and high population counts of 627 and 835 dogs per square mile. The Hopkins study area was estimated to contain 1,270 and 1,690 dogs per square mile, low and high respectively.

Dog Population of the City. To obtain an approximation of the total stray population, we can assume that the main study area contains an average density of free-ranging animals —lower-income areas like the Hopkins area have more dogs and wealthier areas have fewer—so that estimates for this area can be extrapolated for the city as a whole. If there are 450 to 750 free-ranging dogs per square mile in the main study area as indicated by the confidence limits (see Appendix) then there are from 32,400 to 54,000 free-ranging dogs for the 72 square miles of the city. These estimates are one-third to one-half the estimated total dog population (including dogs that are never free-ranging). This is consistent with findings that one-third to one-half of the people who own dogs permit them to run free.

Distribution of Dogs and Socio-economic Characteristics

of Neighborhoods. Two systematic whole city surveys when pooled, revealed that free-ranging dogs were very closely correlated with high-density, low-income areas. With respect to housing, Baltimore remains a largely segregated city, and whereas the distribution of free-ranging dogs fits very closely with the census tracts that are 95% or more black, the small areas inhabited almost exclusively by poor white people also contain free-ranging dogs.

Areas of similar sociological neighborhoods have similar frequencies of free-ranging dogs. In general, the lower half of the city contains the vast majority of free-ranging dogs except for the central business district which, like the wealthier neighborhoods in the north, is relatively free of observable loose dogs.

Discussion

In any animal ecological investigation it is of primary importance to know the number of animals in the study area. Population density is an especially significant parameter when zoonotic diseases are important in the ecology of the system. Estimating the numbers of dogs in an area has always been a major problem for rabies control personnel. Published estimates of total dog population include 500,000 in New York City, 300,000 in Los Angeles (*Time* 1970), 500,000 in Mexico City, 500,000 in Buenos Aires, and 300,000 in Lima (Acha 1969). Schwabe (1969) estimates that in 1966 in the United States there were 24.7 million owned dogs and an undetermined number of ownerless strays. Schwabe also states that over one-half the nation's dogs are in the cities, with 20% to 40% of city families owning at least one dog. From door-to-door interviews, I found dog ownership by family unit ranging from 37% in my main study area to 51% in the Park Circle area.

Most estimates of the dog population of cities in the United States are based on some manipulation of registration figures, or on relating the dog population to the human population, which is sampled much more systematically. Using license or registration figures has obvious failings. Registration is more for taxation than recording dog ownership, although in some areas it provides a way of enforcing required immunizations. Denver increased registration by removing the taxation aspect (Anderson and Cameron 1955).

Kieran (1959) estimated New York City's dog population by multiplying the number of dogs licensed (276,119) by 4.5. In Baltimore it is estimated that no more than 43% of the dogs are licensed (Crawford 1964), but I observed almost no licensing among poor people unless they had to retrieve their dog from the pound, at which time the license law can be enforced. If one assumes that Baltimore's registration of approximately 36,000 dogs represents, at best, 43% of the dog population, then the city has 83,721 dogs.[1]

The other common method of estimating urban dog population is to use the dog-to-human ratio. One of the common estimators, based on the surveys of Marx and Furcolow (1969), assumes that dogs-to-human are in the ratio of 1:7. Using such a fixed ratio has many inherent disadvantages, for it does not take into account the effects of urban human density, published crime rates, fashion, and other parameters known to affect ownership patterns, which, in turn, affect free-ranging dog populations.

If the 1:7 ratio is valid, Baltimore, with its human population of 905,759, has 129,394 dogs. It is interesting to note that seven people represent 2.36 housing units since there are 2.96 people/unit (Census Notes 1971) so that one dog

[1] There is little incentive to register a dog in Baltimore. There is no enforcement of registration laws, and no dog wardens investigate license expiration or stop the owner on the street. There is ordinarily little incentive for rabies immunization, since it is not required by law and since rabies has not been reported in dogs in Baltimore since 1947. (In 1972, however, two one-day rabies immunization centers for dogs and cats were set up in the city because several rabid bats were found in Maryland and in Baltimore itself.)

for seven people is also one dog for 2.36 housing units or 42.4% ownership, which is consistent with my interview estimates of ownership.

Few estimates tackle the problem of whether they are dealing with all dogs in an area, or just owned dogs. Marx and Furcolow (1969) observed a range, in the ratio of un-owned to owned dogs, from 1:2.6 to 1:40.5. I believe that I could not rely on either the registration figure or human population ratio method because Baltimore's human population is decreasing yet the dog population is increasing.

Crawford (1964), using a telephone survey method, estimated that the 1960 dog population in Baltimore was 75,000; and in 1970 he estimated the population at 90,000 (personal communication), a 20% increase; yet the human population decreased by some 33,000 during the same decade.

Despite the obvious drawbacks of using the registration method or the human ratio method, the estimates are roughly consistent with each other. They are also consistent with my estimate of ca. 43,000 free-ranging dogs (which assumes that the total dog population is at least twice this number).

DISTRIBUTION

The reasons for the specific distribution of free-ranging dogs in the city are speculative. Interviews with city officials and residents, and my own observations, suggest that as density goes up so do available garbage, open yards, and more shelter areas for strays. Also, crime rates rise and the social organization of the human residents appears weaker. Higher reported crime rates tend to encourage dog ownership; available garbage attracts and provides food for strays; more open yards mean freer movement for pet dogs; and the many hiding spaces created by the urban renewal of poor areas permit breeding and survival of strays. The looser human social organization inhibits neighbors from putting social pressures on people who let their dogs run free. I found that the people of these areas were less likely to call the municipal animal shelter for pick-up of strays because there is sympathy for dogs, and also because poorer people are not well-informed about city services and how to make use of them.

Ownership of dogs in wealthier neighborhoods is increasing, too, but in these areas people have either enclosed yards or more time to walk their dogs, which are often of a recognizable breed and therefore assumed to be more expensive than the mixed breeds of poorer neighborhoods (Berzon 1971). There are fewer vacant buildings and unused lots and less available garbage in wealthier areas—all factors that tend to discourage proliferation of free-ranging dogs.

The significance of land ownership cannot be ignored as the property or house owner is far more likely to keep his fence repaired and his alley clean than the tenant who lives in a building owned by someone else.

ACTIVITY

During the summer free-ranging dogs are observed in greatest numbers from 0500–0800 hours and 1900–2200 hours, but are almost absent from sight during the heat of the day. At the same time human residents exhibited a slight bimodal pattern peaking at about 1000 and 1900 hours, with least activity from 0100 to 0600 hours (see Fig. 2). The dog's crepuscular pattern is very exaggerated during the summer because of the almost total lack of activity at the hottest times of the day, but during less severe weather some dogs are always active on the streets.

During the summer the numbers of dogs observed was inversely correlated with temperature. Garbage accumulation was associated with increased activity (this will be discussed under "Food Procurement").

The crepuscular activity pattern was observed both in individual dogs living closely with humans (but not living

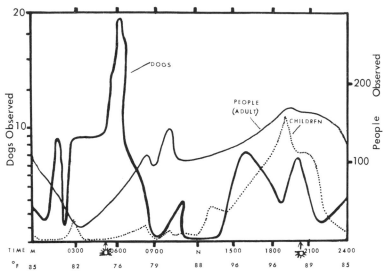

Fig. 2. Dogs and people on the streets in the main study area. The area was surveyed each hour for parts of three consecutive days in June 1970. When the same time of day was sampled twice the results were averaged. Sunset and sunrise are indicated before 0600 and 2100, respectively.

within a dwelling) and in dogs living quite independent of man. Dogs were observed to be released from dwellings during these same activity periods.

Discussion

The absence of dog activity during midday of summer is probably best interpreted as heat avoidance. The early morning and later afternoon activity is both a real pattern as it is observed in animals living without human supervision, and an artifact generated by people's releasing their pets to the streets before and after usual working hours. This flush of pets may also be influencing the dogs already on the streets, since activity appears to stimulate further activity.

During my 14 surveys in 1970 the ambient temperatures ranged from 18.3° to 25.0° C (65° to 77° F) and the numbers of dogs observed ranged from 11 to 31, having a correlation coefficient of 0.566, which is significant at the 0.5 level ($r =$ 0.532) but not at the 0.01 level ($r = 0.661$) with 12 degrees of freedom. There was no obvious correlation between activity and overcast conditions or even slight rain, nor between activity and day of the week (weekends were included in the surveys), so that lessened street activity with increased air temperature seems to be a real phenomenon. Severe cold also lessens street activity, judging from less systematic sampling.

Two dogs, "Shaggy" and "Doberman," observed living outside human dwellings during the population surveys of the main study area were followed on eight different occasions (either throughout their morning or evening activity period) between 29 August and 6 November 1970. Both dogs were adult males. Their use of shelter and their food procurement will be discussed later. Approximately half their morning and evening activity periods were spent resting, much as in case of a well-fed house pet. Figure 3 shows

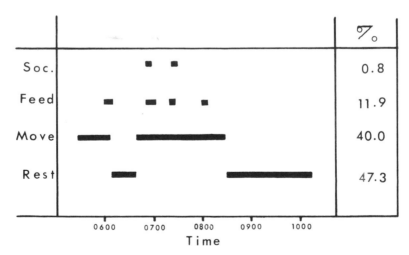

Fig. 3. Four activities of "Shaggy" and "Doberman" during the morning of 2 September 1970. Soc. = social behavior with other dogs, including sniffing and chasing; Feed = feeding behavior, including rummaging through garbage and eating; Move = walking and running; Rest = resting or sleeping.

the time spent in basic activities for a typical day. This typical day has been described in detail elsewhere (Beck 1971). By September 1971 one of the dogs, Shaggy, was adopted and became a house pet, but was still permitted morning and evening runs—an example of a very common activity period, the hour before and after the owner's work schedule.

Continual observations of Tiffany Alley (between Robert and Presstman Streets in the main study area) revealed that there is some dog activity all through the night. This alley was observed because it contained a female with young pups; they, too, showed some activity at odd hours in the night. The alley became noticeably more active during the peak periods previously discussed. The resident dogs were always active during the peaks and there were many more visits from other dogs of the area during these periods. Ducatel Alley (between Whitelock and Ducatel Streets) was also studied and showed similar trends.

It was convenient to study the dog population immediately surrounding The Johns Hopkins School of Hygiene and Public Health during the winter (throughout the month of February 1971). Activity peaks similar to the summer schedule were observed; however, the dogs remained active until 1130 instead of 0900 as during the summer. Snow on the ground did not appear to reduce activity.

From 21 July to 4 August 1971 I observed the activity of a truly feral pack, living in forest land in the Chapel Gate Road area. These dogs lived free from any human dwelling. The same crepuscular activity peaks prevailed (see Fig. 2) that were observed with the previously discussed dogs; that is, the feral dogs usually did not come into open grounds for running and garbage feeding until sunrise and they appeared again at sunset. This group also showed some activity at night. They made only sporadic appearances during the day. Their activity was not completely divorced from human patterns; their raiding of garbage cans was not tolerated by the residents of the area, and the dogs were often chased by people playing on the college grounds. It was their apparently retaliatory chasing of people that eventually led to their demise, to be discussed later.

It is not clear how much dog activity is inherent to the species of *Canis* under consideration and how much is related to man's influence; but it is obvious that man is very much part of the ecology of the dog. There are similar examples elsewhere, e.g., Barbehenn's (1969) work with small mammals, where one animal's activity is very much influenced by another species living in the same community.

LAND USE PATTERNS

Free-ranging dogs primarily use alleyways for most behaviors, including resting, moving from place to place, feeding, and mating; 40% of all dogs observed were in alleys. Streets and sidewalks were used only half as much for the same behaviors during morning activity periods (Table 1). During this period, moving was the most common behavior; 68% of all dogs were observed to be in transit and nearly 38% of all such dogs were in transit in alleys. Resting was the second most frequently observed behavior, occurring about equally in alleys, sidewalks, streets, and lots (unpaved open areas). While only 11% of the dogs were observed to be engaged in food procurement, 88% of those procuring food were in alleys, and the rest were seen equally on streets, sidewalks, and lots. All social behavior was observed in the streets.

Nearly half the leashed dogs were walked on sidewalks and only 18% in the streets. An additional 9% were being walked in parks and playgrounds.

Discussion

Table 1 is primarily a first approximation of land use patterns. It is based on where dogs were seen during 14 con-

Table 1. Land use patterns for specific behaviors
(14 daily morning observation periods, Summer, 1971)

Location	N	%	House porch	Steps or sidewalk	Street	Yard	Alley	Park or playground	Lot	Other[a]
% of all dogs[b]										
Resting	44	19.2	2.2	3.9	3.5	0.4	4.4	1.7	3.1	0.0
Moving	156	68.0	1.3	14.8	16.6	0.0	25.7	2.2	7.0	0.4
Feeding	25	11.0	0.0	0.4	0.4	0.0	9.6	0.0	0.4	0.0
Socializing	2	0.9	0.0	0.0	0.9	0.0	0.0	0.0	0.0	0.0
Mating	2	0.9	0.0	0.0	0.0	0.0	0.4	0.4	0.0	0.0
TOTALS	229	100.0	3.5	19.1	21.4	0.4	40.1	4.3	10.5	0.4
% of those dogs[c]										
Resting	44	100.0	11.4	20.4	18.2	2.3	22.7	9.1	16.0	0.0
Moving	156	100.0	1.9	14.8	21.8	0.0	37.7	3.2	10.3	0.6
Feeding	25	100.0	0.0	4.0	4.0	0.0	88.0	0.0	4.0	0.0
Socializing	2	100.0	0.0	0.0	100.0	0.0	0.0	0.0	0.0	0.0
Mating	2	100.0	0.0	0.0	0.0	0.0	0.4	0.4	0.0	0.0
Being walked	66	100.0	0.0	45.5	18.2	0.0	16.7	9.1	10.6	0.0

[a] Paved open areas, such as parking lots.
[b] Percentage based on total number (229) of observed free-roving dogs.
[c] Percentage based on totals (N) for each behavioral category.

secutive morning surveys that were taken during the summer
of 1971 in the main study area. The relative surface areas
of the different land features, e.g., streets and alleys, were not
measured, but subjectively streets represent the most available space, followed by sidewalks, alleys and lots. Even though
alleys do not contain the most available open space, they
were the most used by dogs for all behavioral categories, with
streets being second. Alleys were less traveled by cars and
people, and contained the greatest stores of food. The dog's
preference for alleys may be a response to pedestrian traffic,
as people use sidewalks more than streets, and streets more
than alleys (P. Williamson, personal communication). Of
course, dogs and people often use the same space.

People primarily walked their dogs on the sidewalk.
Baltimore does not have a law requiring dogs to be walked
in the streets ("curb law"), thus pedestrian pathways and tree
areas adjacent to streets receive a heavy fecal load from pet
dogs, the implications of which will be discussed later. Playgrounds specifically designed for children were used as dog
walking areas by 9% of the observed pet owners, indicating
a disregard for the value of clean play areas for children.

HOME RANGE

The home range of two dogs, Shaggy and Doberman,
was determined by direct observation. When they were free-
ranging for the entire day, the range was approximately 2.59
hectare (0.1 square mile) (see Fig. 4). After Shaggy became
a well-cared-for house pet, released only for short periods
daily, his range was no more than 0.52 hectare (0.02 square
mile). Shaggy was able to return to his house area after being
released some 6.4 km (4 miles) away (see p. 21). The range of
the Hopkins area group, which was entirely free-ranging but
had human food (through handouts) and shelter available,
was approximately 1.5 hectare (0.06 square mile). The ranges

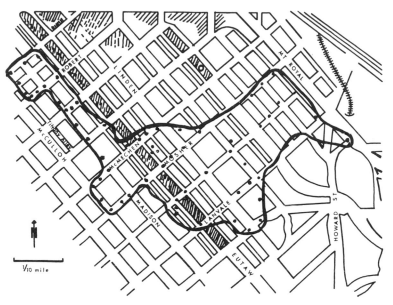

Fig. 4. Home range of "Shaggy" and "Doberman." Dots indicate places frequently visited by the dogs. Shaded areas are park-like areas with trees or grass.

did not appear to conform to prominent boundaries such as major street crossings or fields.

Discussion

The home range of a free-ranging dog appears to resemble closely the "home range" conceptualized by Burt (1943)—"an area, usually around a homesite, over which the animal usually travels in search of food." Dogs spend much of their time near the center of the range. They do not protect the central area from conspecifics, as observed with true territories. Some territorial behavior was observed when a female had pups under a porch; she would chase other females out of the alley near the porch. As Scott and Fuller (1965) observed in their studies, even free-ranging dogs that have no need to hunt or scavange for food make regular journeys within their range, frequently marking enroute.

The home range for two dogs, Shaggy and Doberman, is irregularly shaped (Fig. 4) with extensions to open fields and feeding sites, which are alleys containing garbage. Movements of these dogs on a typical morning appear to outline an ameboid-shaped area typical of many mammalian home ranges (Burt 1943). The area does not have the biases attributed to ranges derived from trapping data (Hayne 1949; Adams and Davis 1967), since multiple sightings were possible within short periods of time. Actually, the data are similar to those gathered with the aid of telemetry systems. Adams and Davis (1967) believed direct observation gives a more accurate description of home range than do capture-recapture methods. The recapture photos I used for population abundance were labeled by location; they were first used as if they were "trap" recapture records and were analyzed for home range information. The estimates were much smaller than those derived from continuous observation of individuals, thus validating the usual criticisms of trap data methods of home range estimation. Fortunately, the urban dog is an excellent model for continuous observation, even without telemetry.

A similar method of plotting was applied to a pack which was followed through February 1970 in the Hopkins study area. This study was not as extensive as with Shaggy and Doberman, but the pack was never seen nor reported to me outside of a 1.5 hectare (0.06 square mile) area. Various changes obviated a comparison of the two groups for both summer and winter. The Hopkins area group of four, varying in body size, though generally smaller than Shaggy and Doberman, were "pets" of the block, i.e., they were fed on occasion and even rescued from the animal shelter. They were, however, routinely free-ranging on the streets all day. I feel that more food was available to them than for Shaggy and Doberman. It is tempting to hypothesize that the smaller home range of this pack (compared to the home range for Shaggy and Doberman) is related to more food's being available to them and not to their slightly smaller body size or to seasonal differences. Some evidence stems from the observation that when Shaggy was adopted by an area resident and became a well-cared-for pet, permitted to run free during the usual A.M. and P.M. activity periods, his range dropped to no more than 0.52 hectare (0.02 square mile) and he spent most of his time within 30.5 m (100 feet) of his owner's door.

Home range is probably influenced by food availability for many animals (McNab 1963). Ables (1969) observed that red foxes, *Vulpes vulpes*, had smaller ranges in areas of great ecological diversity compared with foxes in suboptimal habitat. Future investigations on the bioenergetics of free-ranging dogs would prove fascinating, but would be a real challenge, for the dog derives much of his energy input from man's civilization, e.g., heated buildings and food handouts, items difficult to quantify.

Each of my studies of home range involved more than one dog, and it should be noted that the observations are not independent ones, since each dog's movements are likely to influence the movements of another dog. There is a social facilitation effect as dogs move or rest. Indeed, group action may influence many behaviors of wolves and dogs (Scott and Fuller 1965). Also, the home range given indicates total surface area included within the outermost excursions and does not represent the actual area available to the dogs, such as some buildings. The city is a three dimensional structure for those dogs who can climb steps and utilize upper floors and roofs of some buildings.

One interesting event that demonstrates the homing abilities of the urban dog deserves reporting here as part of the home-range concept. After the Shaggy was adopted, he was brought by automobile to his owner's mother, who lived nearly 6.4 km (4 miles) to the northeast. The dog ran away and returned home within 2.5 hours. I had been studying Shaggy throughout the summer and I knew that he never ventured that far. (I believe that releasing dogs in the city for experimental purposes is unsafe for people and dogs, so homing experiments were not undertaken.)

The home ranges included here are smaller than those reported for dogs in rural areas (M. Douglas Scott 1971, and W. Harold Nesbitt, personal communication, working in Alabama and Illinois, respectively). Probably rural dogs have to range further to obtain food. Shaggy's small range and short activity period may indicate a favorable habitat in Baltimore for free-ranging dogs.

FOOD AND WATER PROCUREMENT

Although some active predation may occur on rats in city alleys and on birds in urban wooded areas, free-ranging urban dogs find food chiefly in garbage and human handouts. People have been observed putting food out for dogs, and this activity has been confirmed by interview. There is a slight decrease in the number of animals observed on the first day after garbage collection and each morning thereafter until the third day. The mean number of dogs observed ($N = 8$) in several 1/8 square mile areas during my morning surveys was 9.5 on the day garbage was collected. The next day the mean fell to 8.0, and then climbed on the two subsequent days to 9.4 and 11.8.

Water is available in gutters and in sidewalk puddles filled by rain, car washing, leaking fire hydrants, and air conditioning units. Water supply may be a problem for short periods during the hot summer days between rain storms, though water almost always appeared to be available during my surveys.

Discussion

Many free-ranging dogs are house pets released for only part of the day, and presumably are fed by their owners, but these dogs, as well as dogs that are not fed by people, find food by rummaging through garbage. Almost all free-ranging urban dogs find some edible food by going through trash cans. Dogs can tip over garbage cans and boxes, open paper and plastic bags containing garbage, and are often observed carrying such bags back to protected areas where careful rummaging takes place. The problems related to this garbage scattering will be discussed later with other public health implications. It is not clear whether dogs can smell food in plastic bags or whether they have learned that food is there from previous encounters with open bags.

One ecological parameter with several implications is the effect of trash collection on free-ranging dogs. I estimated the effects by counting the numbers of free-ranging dogs

As they search for food, free-ranging dogs commonly overturn garbage cans, thus making food easily available for rats and also increasing the cost of trash collection.

within one-eighth square mile areas on the day of garbage
collection and for the next three days, since it was not possible to undertake a controlled experiment. Presumably
there are more dogs where food is more abundant, and the
slight variations in the mean number of dogs that I observed
(from 9.5 down to 8 following garbage collection, and up
within two days to nearly 12) probably reflect changes in the
availability of the dogs' chief food supply—garbage—in the
city. (The number of observed animals has been used to
indicate habitat preference of non-urban animals like deer
[Vogl and Beck 1970].)

There is some evidence here that dogs might be used as
indicators of environmental deterioration, since their presence is generally correlated with excessive garbage, which in
turn is presumably correlated with rat density. Using dogs
(which are easily sampled) as indicators could help to show
the effectiveness of rat eradication efforts, and might help
to increase the efficiency of rat control programs, especially
if dogs were associated with rats for other reasons to be
discussed later.

One reason that the shifts in the numbers of dogs after
collection are not more significant is that there is often ample
litter left on the ground after trash collection. Trash that
is already on the ground (as from garbage cans previously
disrupted by dogs) is not collected until street sweepers come
through on days other than collection days (see photos). Additional sweepings financed by federal funds may change dog
patterns, but the clean-up is too new for any comments at
this time.

The presence of free-ranging dogs in poorer neighborhoods is probably correlated with the excessive garbage readily available in these areas. This excessive garbage appears
to arise from (i) the high density of people in poor neighborhoods; (ii) the fact that there are only two weekly pick-ups
of refuse regardless of density; (iii) the concentration of garbage cans in narrow alleys behind the row houses; (iv) lack

Dogs roam the alleys before trash is collected and return immediately afterward to scavenge garbage spilled or left behind.

of provision for preventing trash cans, often without covers, from being knocked over by dogs; (v) inadequate number of cans; (vi) lack of proper motivation to police alleys or enforce litter codes, since residents are not the landowners; (vii) dumpster doors often being difficult to open in city projects where dumpsters are used, so that garbage is left outside the dumpster; and (viii) lack of garbage disposal units in high-density areas.

I believe scavanging to be the primary food-procuring mechanism of roaming urban dogs; however, some active predation does occur. For example, the dogs that lived in the woods in the Chapel Gate area reportedly killed ground-nesting birds, and I have one report of a dog that killed rats. (Dogs killed 49 animals one night at the Baltimore Zoo though the dead animals were not eaten [R. Thompson, personal communication].)

Food is also available to strays through the kindness of area residents. Food left out for any dog was discovered by free-ranging dogs both in the main study area and in the Hopkins area. In addition, food may be given to specific stray dogs though these dogs are not house pets. The Shaggy and Doberman were fed somewhat regularly by a woman who dropped food from a second floor window (see photo). These dogs often waited for this food. I interviewed every head of household ($N = 38$), usually female, who was home along a block that cut through a very low-income area and 20% of those interviewed had observed people putting food out for dogs or had done so themselves. This phenomenon was uncommon in the middle class residential Windsor Hills area (with comparable dog density). (In this case the information was gathered by a "show of hands" at a neighborhood association meeting ($N = 20$) and comparison may not be valid.)

Shaggy and Doberman never spent more than 11% of any activity period in direct food procurement behavior. It is interesting to note that when Shaggy was taken in as a house pet, after spending all summer as a totally free-ranging

A free-ranging dog—"Shaggy" (see also Figs. 3 and 4)—gets his regular handout from a sympathetic resident of a second floor apartment.

dog, he weighed 15.9 kg (35 lbs). After six weeks of being the pampered pet of a wealthy bachelor he weighed only 16.3 kg (36 lbs), indicating that he was quite capable of maintaining his body weight from garbage and handouts.

Except for "worms" and ear mites the owner's veterinarian considered the dog in good health.

Noticeably thin street dogs are often animals suffering from disease, indicated by dripping mouths, noses, or eyes. In general, street dogs appear to receive adequate food. They are easily able to disperse rats and cats, and may be the apex consumers of garbage in the urban ecosystem. (Only once have I observed a human being going through garbage, and he probably was not looking for food.) As mentioned above, the small home range and the limited activity of dogs observed in this study probably indicate a more-than-adequate food supply.

Water appeared to be always available as it accumulated in gutters and sidewalk puddles. Shaggy and Doberman frequently used the runoff from a leaking air conditioning unit. At one point during a hot dry spell the dogs in the Hopkins study area were routinely observed visiting a drain which usually contained water on the lawn of The Johns Hopkins Hospital. They eventually found a leaking fire hydrant a block away and began making frequent trips to the adjacent gutter which had become a tiny stream. Water also was supplied by humans, as with food, and free-ranging dogs have been observed benefiting from the food and water left in backyards for owned pets. Rats, too, have been seen making use of these same backyard food and water sources.

SHELTER

The urban environment contains numerous areas where dogs can find cover and protection against adverse weather conditions, people, and other dogs. These areas are used for resting, sleeping, and whelping.

Sites offering complete cover include vacant buildings and garages, as well as those under construction, and hallways of occupied buildings. There are also topographic features in the environment that offer some protection against rain, wind, heat, and cold. These include dense shrubbery around buildings, in woodlots, and under porch steps. Dogs show various forms of heat avoidance behavior, such as sleeping under parked cars during the day, and insulating themselves from the hot or wet ground by resting on top of discarded mattresses, and on roofs of parked cars (see photo).

Diverse features, such as parked cars in urban environment, can provide shade (*top*) or insulation from the ground. The dog below habitually slept on top of this car, as shown. He is pictured here just before jumping down in the morning.

Resting in tree plots has been observed, and digging holes in backyards and resting on tops of gravestones has been reported to me. In one area the complex topography of a landfill area which turned into a dump was used extensively by dogs for shelter and socializing.

Discussion

There are over 16,000 vacant buildings in Baltimore (Census Notes 1971). In the name of urban renewal, the city's Department of Housing and Community Development has condemned houses all over the row-house area in the southern half of the city, and these are used extensively by dogs, according to Housing Authority photographers who have inspected them. I accompanied the photographers on two different occasions and found either dog signs—usually feces —or the dogs themselves in about half of the houses we entered. We could not enter most of the buildings because they were boarded up, were unsafe, or had too much litter within them, but many boarded buildings inaccessible to people had sufficient access for dogs.

Buildings that were being built in the main study area were used extensively by dogs during the winter of 1970, and workmen routinely had to chase dogs out at the beginning of each work day.

The boarding up of buildings and their eventual clearing raises interesting ecological questions regarding the fate of the dogs that use them. During February 1970 I followed six animals using three vacant buildings in the Hopkins area. When one of the buildings was totally boarded the pack simply moved over to an open one. The buildings were wrecked over a period of a few weeks. All during the period while some rubble remained, the dogs continued to use the area. I could find them at night sleeping in the rubble even though they no longer had total cover. Once the area was cleared they moved to another building across the alley. At first I could not find them, but the residents knew of their move. Within two months, three of the six dropped out of sight. One was found dead in the street four blocks away, within their collective home range, an apparent car kill. Will urban renewal increase dog mortality? Will it push dogs into new areas, and possibly affect disease and bite patterns? Similar questions can be raised regarding dumps and landfills, which are also used by dogs. In Washington, D.C., the Kenilworth landfill was cleared and the dogs that previously lived in the trash remained to terrorize local residents. Reports of dogs chasing and biting people continued even though the food was gone (Hebald 1969).

In the Park Circle area of Baltimore, the local dump was studied by direct observation and interviews of people living on the dump's periphery. The area was a sanitary landfill but soon became a dumping ground for trash and large bulk items like furniture and automobiles. Dogs could be routinely observed socializing and resting amidst the cover of the complex topography. I felt unsafe walking through the area at night, for the presence of wild dogs shifting about and barking was unnerving. High-power strobe photos revealed heavy dog use. During the study the area was bulldozed clean but a planned fence never materialized and the dogs were never really displaced. Future slum and dump clearance should consider the fate of the dogs displaced for the sake of the animals and of the people in the cleared areas.

Buildings occupied by people are also used by free-ranging dogs. Shaggy used an occupied building for a while, by pushing the front door open to gain entrance and waiting for someone to leave to get back to the street. While in the building he slept, fed, and "marked" in an area under the stairway. Eventually the odor got so bad that he was chased out by the superintendent. He then, with the Doberman, began using shrubbery around a business building. The dense shrubbery afforded cover that kept the dogs out of sight and was cooler and dryer than the adjacent concrete sidewalk.

A back staircase is part of every row house. Under this and the accompanying porch is a shaded area often used by pet and free-ranging dogs. In one case I observed, such an area was used for whelping a litter of six. The pups could join their mother in the alley for food. The porch helped keep the dogs out of sight and afforded shade from the summer sun.

The dogs that lived on the grounds of the abandoned Paulist College lived and whelped in a hardwood stand that was several acres in area. At least six dogs and an unknown number of pups found cover in this wooded lot.

Dogs, like wolves (Scott and Fuller 1965), rarely alter their environment (like digging a den) to produce cover, but use what is available for concealment. During my interviews I had several reports of free-ranging dogs digging holes in back yards to get to cooler soil for resting; but I found most heat avoidance behavior directed toward finding cooler places rather than toward actual manipulation of the environment. The urban environment contains many such places for dogs who are tolerant of human proximity and, more important, who are tolerated by proximate humans. If dogs were not so accepted as part of the city, their shelter-seeking activity would be wholly different—probably more like that of rats, who can never use parked cars or mattresses exposed to human view.

SOCIAL ORGANIZATION

Free-ranging dogs often occur in groups, the sizes of which are not random, but indicate some social interaction. One-half the dogs reported on in this study were observed as singles, nearly 26% in pairs, about 16% in groups of three, and 7% in groups of four or five (Table 2). The mean size of groups was 2.46 dogs. Sporadically, larger groups are seen. I saw groups as large as 17 dogs, and larger packs have been reported to me. Most groups vary as to size and membership; few groups appear stable. At any one time, a leader is usually discernible. The groups are composed of dogs of varying breeds, sizes, and temperaments. Ninety percent of the dogs brought to the Hopkins Medical Institutions from the Animal Shelter are classified as mongrels; they vary considerably with regard to coat type, tail length, and weight. It is obvious that the free-ranging dog population is a very heterogeneous one.

The morning population surveys showed that the frequencies of group sizes (Table 2) were not what one might

Table 2. Frequency of group size in stray dogs
(from 28 surveys of a one-fourth square mile plot).

Group size	No. of groups observed	No. of dogs involved	% of dogs involved
1	270	270	50.6
2	69	138	25.9
3	29	87	16.3
4	7	28	5.3
5	2	10	1.9
	377	533	100.0

expect if the dogs were grouped at random. Random grouping would occur if there were no social behaviors that would tend to either clump or disperse the animals any more than would be expected from chance encounters during the survey periods (J. E. Cohen 1971, and personal communication). (For statistical discussion, see Appendix.)

Discussion

It is interesting to note that the number of pairs of dogs observed, 69, was only three-quarters of what would be expected, ca. 94, if the dogs were distributed randomly. Possible explanations include: female-female pairs were never observed (which would account for one-quarter of all pairs if the sex ratio was unity), or mated pairs may spend less time on the streets. The effects of sex composition within the groups remains to be studied.

Groups form and dissolve as new dogs run with the group for a while and then leave. Although some individual groups were stable, like the Shaggy and Doberman pair, the core group of four in the Hopkins area, and the pack that lived in the woods on the abandoned Paulist College, my findings agree with Scott and Fuller's (1965, p. 62) description of dog social organization: "Except where they are allowed to run wild, domestic dogs rarely form stable packs, although dogs in a neighborhood sometimes join together and run in temporary groups." Stable, and larger packs of five or six are observed in dogs free-running in rural areas; these dogs also appear to be more morphologically uniform than urban dogs (P. Scott 1971; Perry and Giles 1970; H. Nesbitt personal communication). Wolves form even larger packs, up to 20 to 24 (Mech 1966).

An overwhelming first impression one gets from observing Baltimore's street dogs is the lack of morphological and behavioral uniformity. The absence of purebreds is indicated by noting that 45% of reported dog bites come from mongrels (D. Berzon, personal communication) and 90% of the Animal Shelter dogs that arrive at Hopkins for research are classified as mongrels. King (1954), working with captive purebreds, found that strangers of the same sex and breed were more likely to be aggressively rejected from social groups than dogs of different sex and breed. This could account for the smaller more transient groups and the high social tolerance observed in Baltimore's free-ranging dog population.

Dogs vary not only with regard to breed, but body size, shape and temperament. This variability, in addition to helping to explain the small transient group sizes observed, may even help to explain the large population of dogs, for the variability reduces competition for food and shelter resources, and increases the carrying capacity of the area. Thus, I have observed larger dogs knocking over garbage cans and making food available for smaller dogs.

Also, dogs vary considerably in their wariness of people and new situations; so some dogs feed while people are present while others wait until they are undisturbed; some dogs will investigate a vacant building whereas others will not. In addition people prefer to feed some dogs more than others because of their appearance or behavior. There does not appear to be a selection for any one physical or behavioral attribute, but rather a place for all. The observed morphological and behavioral variations are either a real biological phenomenon serving some adaptive function at the population level or a fortuitous result of man's capricious manipulation of inherent canine variability. In any case, the variations are conducive to a loose social structure with small transient groups and a greater utilization of the habitat's resources.

MORTALITY

Death comes to free-ranging urban dogs primarily from disease, collisions with automobiles, being collected by the Animal Shelter and subsequently disposed of, or being killed intentionally by human beings acting without public sanction. Death from starvation, cold, or exposure appears to be rare. From July 1970 to June 1971 (one year) 8,394 dead dogs were removed from Baltimore city streets; most were probably killed by cars and disease. During the same period, the Animal Shelter collected or received 18,557 dogs and puppies of which 15,380 were gassed or sent to medical institutions (Table 3). The total known mortality for the year was 23,773 animals, or nearly 24% of the estimated popu-

Table 3. Sources of mortality indicated by Animal Shelter records

Sources	1969–70 [a]	1970–71 [a]
Gassed dogs	7,170	9,632
Gassed pups	2,370	2,662
10-day gassed dogs [b]	321	424
10-day gassed pups [b]	16	10
10-day dogs that died during observation period [b]	208	29
Requisitioned by hospitals [c]	3,398	2,622
Subtotal (shelter death)	13,483	15,379
Dead animals collected from streets	8,394	8,394
Total (mortality)	21,877	23,773

[a] Each interval is from July to June, one year.

[b] Animals held for ten days for observation for rabies after biting a human being.

[c] Included under "Sources of mortality" since these animals are removed from the street population.

lation. This is an increase of 8.6% in the known mortality from the previous year. (For comparison, all known indices of street cat mortality, e.g., number dead on streets and numbers brought to the Shelter and gassed, also showed increases.)

Approximately half of the dead dogs sampled were under the mean age of 2.3 years for males and 2.6 years for females. (In many wildlife species, females tend to live longer than males.) Dividing an entry in the $1000q_x$ column of Table 4 by 10 gives the percent mortality for that age interval. One can see that 44.9% of the population theoretically dies the first year; totaling the first two entries in the d_x column reveals that 60.3% of the population dies before reaching the mean age of 2.3 years. (See also Fig. 5.)

The age structure of the population is very much part of the mortality picture. In 1970–71 the pound disposed of over 15,000 animals and collected another 8,000 from the streets, giving a known mortality of 23% of the population (see Table 3). This is a very conservative estimate, since not every dead animal is found; indeed, only those dead in the

Table 4. Life table for free-roving dogs based on the known age at death of dogs dying between April and September 1971

	x	l_x	d_x	$1,000q_x$	e_x
Total	0–1 [a]	1,000	449	449	2.3
$N = 78$	1–2	551	154	279	2.8
$x = 2.31$	2–3	397	51	128	2.7
	3–4	346	64	185	2.0
	4–5	282	103	365	1.3
	5–6	179	123	687	0.8
	6–7	56	56	1,000	0.5
			1,000		

Legend: x = age interval in years; l_x = number surviving at beginning of age interval/1,000; d_x = number dying in age interval/1,000; $1,000q_x$ = mortality rate/1,000 alive at beginning of age interval, and e_x = expectation of life, or mean life-time remaining to those attaining age interval.

[a] Undoubtedly an underestimate due to sample bias.

Note: Mean age is 2.31 years for males and 2.62 years for females.

open on public property are counted. Dead dogs disappear in a few days if not collected, either destroyed by traffic or by natural decay (microorganisms and insects). A mortality of 50% does not seem unreasonable, and such a rapid turn-over means a younger population.

Discussion

In general, dogs found dead on the streets had a shorter life span than the usual pet. (A survey of household pets in Denver showed a mean age of 10.5 years, with only 18.6% of the pet dogs below age 3 (Univ. Denver 1952). Dorn, Ter-brush, and Hibbard (1967) in a thorough study of household pets in California found a mean age of 4.4 years, with more than half being under 3 years, and a male:female ratio of 49:51.) The ages of dead dogs brought in from the streets by the Animal Shelter were determined during this study by examining the teeth. Baltimore's free-ranging dogs suffer a higher mortality than pets, with a mean age of 2.3 years.

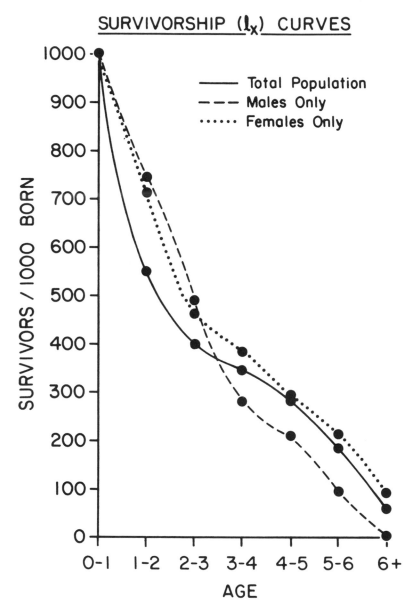

Fig. 5. Length of life of free-ranging dogs in Baltimore. (See also Table 4.)

A concerned crowd formed immediately after this dog had been injured by a hit-and-run automobile driver. A police officer (in dark trousers, standing in the street facing the dog) stayed with the animal until shelter personnel arrived, both to help prevent traffic tie-ups and to discourage bystanders from handling the animal (since injured dogs tend to bite).

In my sample taken from dead dogs, I found a male:female ratio of 64:36, possibly indicating a differential mortality. Pound dogs brought to Johns Hopkins Hospital for research have a sex ratio of 1:1, but these are both free-ranging dogs from the streets and unwanted house pets that had been turned in to the shelter.

The rapid population turnover indicated by the high mortality and substantiated by the lowering of mean age has many epidemiological implications. A young population of new individuals would be more susceptible to diseases such as rabies and distemper and to worm infestations, such as by *Toxocara canis*. Also, younger dogs bite more often than older ones. All of these problems will be discussed in detail later.

The Animal Shelter. The Municipal Animal Shelter is the primary agency concerned with dog control in Baltimore, and the only organization that actively collects dead and live animals from the streets. The private organizations in the city, i.e., the S.P.C.A., the Anti-Vivisection Society, the Workers for Animal Protection, Inc., and nearly 30 registered practicing veterinarians also handle live and dead animals, but these are almost exclusively pets and presumably a dog owner who avails himself of these services is not so

likely to own a free-ranging animal. For this reason, and
since the private societies were not particularly cooperative
during my study, only the pound's records will be discussed
as sources of insight into free-ranging dogs.

The Animal Shelter operates at least two trucks from
0830 to 1530 hours for the retrieval of live animals (emergency service) and two trucks for collecting dead animals
(scavenger service). Emergency service mainly includes an-
swering house calls to collect sick, "not wanted," and stray
dogs. The strays are usually gone by the time the truck
arrives, though workers often stop to pursue strays while en
route from house to house. The scavenger trucks, too, respond mainly to calls; they stop if a dead animal is sighted.
The police call for service when confronted with vicious
animals or dead or injured dogs. Calls are relayed to the
trucks via civil band radio shared with several other city
services. Emergency trucks operate every day but Sunday.
After 1600 hours and all day Sunday a single truck operates
to collect dead animals and respond to emergencies (sick or
vicious dogs), and to collect biters. Basically, there is 24-hour
service. People bring animals directly to the shelter as well
as buy animals there at a minimal cost. Strays are held for
7 days during which time they may be redeemed by owners
before they are put up for adoption, sold to medical institutions, or gassed. Animals are killed with water-cooled carbon
monoxide gas exhausted from an internal combustion engine.

I have traveled with emergency and scavenger trucks on
all shifts. The emergency trucks travel some 70–100 miles of
streets bringing in from 20 to 50 dogs per day, mostly sick,
injured, and unwanted ones. The heavy load of calls prevents
emphasis on chasing strays. I have observed people harassing
the dog catchers by cursing them and by chasing away dogs.
Every time I went out with the trucks there were some situations which required police involvement. There were cases
of animals that were victims of human cruelty, including
stabbings and burnings. Some isolated incidents while I was
with the truck included catching extremely vicious dogs,

releasing dogs that were boarded up in a building, retrieving very sick dogs, and having to gas a dog that was hit by a car at night when no veterinarian was on duty.

Scavenger service lacks the excitement of the chase and is involved mainly with finding the animal once the truck arrives in the general area of a call. The dead animals together with the dogs killed at the pound and the S.P.C.A. are taken to a rendering plant outside the city where meat and bone scrap (with a crude protein content of not less than 50%) is prepared and sold as chicken and hog food supplement. The grease is used in the manufacture of low phosphate soaps. This is one of the few examples of recycling of natural components in the urban ecosystem.

Table 5 shows yearly totals for various pound activities. Dogs and puppies "received" represents all dogs brought to the pound. A definite increase in pound activities dealing with dogs can be noted. The "other" animals representing the city's wildlife, including opossums, raccoons, squirrels, and some exotic pets, are decreasing in numbers. Other indicators of a possibly increasing dog population are the noticeable increases in calls, especially for strays and "10-day" dogs. (The latter are biters and will be discussed below with the dog-bite problem.) Table 3 lists only sources of mortality. The sharp increase (34.3%) in the numbers of dogs gassed could indicate not only the increase in the numbers received but also the decrease in the numbers requisitioned for medical research. This decrease may reflect the decreased funding for medical research experienced by many local institutions. The reasons for the apparently unchanged numbers of scavenged animals are not clear, though they may reflect decreased pound effort due to numerous truck problems during part of the year.

During the last three decades the number of dogs received at the shelter has increased continuously. The number of dogs sold is increasing; and the number of dogs redeemed by owners apparently is increasing.

One useful insight into the natural history of the urban

Table 5. Some Indices of Animal Shelter Activity over a 3-Year Period

	1968–69 [a]	1969–70	1970–71
Received [b]			
Dogs	14,114	16,736	18,557
Cats	1,680	2,036	2,191
Others [c]	108	92	71
10-day [d]			
Dogs	346	611	632
Cats	40	49	74
Redeemed			
Dogs	—[e]	751	857
10-day dogs	—[e]	208	192
Sold			
Dogs	2,060	2,028	2,110
Gassed			
Dogs	7,974	9,540	12,294
Cats	1,667	1,754	2,109
Dead animals from the			
streets			
Dogs	8,605	8,394	8,394
Cats	5,012	4,690	5,123
Telephone calls			
Unwanted dogs	14,870	15,845	18,919
Stray dogs	3,896	3,745	4,429

[a] Each interval is from July to June, one year.

[b] All animals that were brought to the shelter by individuals or dog catchers.

[c] Mainly opossums, squirrels, raccoons, and exotic pets.

[d] Animals held for 10 days for observation for rabies after biting a person.

[e] Figures not available.

dog is revealed by the pound's monthly records. Figure 6 shows that most dogs arrive at the pound during the summer, whereas most puppies arrive in the fall and winter.

Dog sales at the pound increased during November and January of 1970–71, and puppy sales increased during all three years (1968–71), which may indicate that dogs are used as gifts for Christmas. In the last two years there also has been an increase in the numbers of dogs and of puppies sold during March, just before the Easter holiday. Distinguishing between human behavioral patterns and ecological influences on the dog population may prove to be a formidable task!

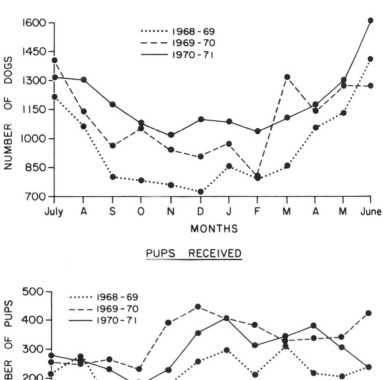

DOGS RECEIVED

········ 1968-69
––– 1969-70
——— 1970-71

NUMBER OF DOGS

MONTHS

PUPS RECEIVED

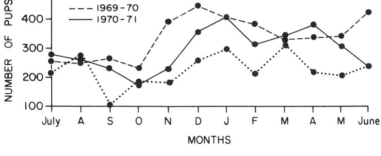

········ 1968-69
––– 1969-70
——— 1970-71

NUMBER OF PUPS

MONTHS

CATS RECEIVED

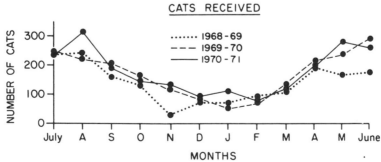

········ 1968-69
––– 1969-70
——— 1970-71

NUMBER OF CATS

MONTHS

Fig. 6. Dogs, pups, and cats received by the Animal Shelter. Monthly totals are plotted for three years.

43

Scavenger activity varied from year to year, possibly indicating that there are many factors, including variations in local climate and in pound effort, that influence the number of deceased animals brought in.

Cat activity is shown for comparison (Table 5 and Figure 6). Stray cats are not actively collected by the pound, so only animals brought to the pound and picked up by the scavenger service are shown. In both categories there is a decrease of activity during the winter, giving only an annual peak during the summer.

One thing is clear—if the city had funds to keep records for many years and a secretarial staff to compile them accurately, these records could be used to plan a more efficient dog management program.

Most dogs examined at the Municipal Animal Shelter appear, from their poor and yellowed teeth, to have been exposed to distemper. Chief Veterinarian for Maryland's Health Department, Dr. Kenneth Crawford, feels that of all dogs born in the city only one out of four will survive eight months, primarily due to distemper and other diseases (Large 1971), which is a slightly lower survival rate than I observed.

An interesting insight into dog control was acquired when the dogs living on the abandoned college in the Chapel Gate area became a local nuisance by chasing people playing on the grounds. The Shelter was unable to catch the animals on the open fields and the police was unwilling to shoot them or let others do so. I was given "unofficial" permission to try trapping, i.e., the police agreed to "look the other way." I caught two dogs in three trap nights. A local resident anxious to hunt and impatient with my success finally secured "unofficial" permission to shoot them. Two dogs were shot one morning and the remaining pack of four dispersed, an incident which indicates the possibilities of new sources of mortality and of new control methods when a dog problem becomes serious.

CHAPTER THREE

Public Health Aspects

DOG BITE

Frequency

In 1969 Baltimore had 6,415 reported animal bites of which 6,023 were dog bites; and in 1970 there were 7,313 animal bites of which 6,809 were dog bites (D. Berzon et al. 1972). The number of bites since 1960 has increased 54.3%, even though the dog population increased only 20% and the human population decreased. The animal bite rate per 100,000 increased from 425 in 1970 to 737 in 1971.

Over the years about 25% of the bites were from stray animals, and over 90% of these strays were dogs. In city health reports, "stray" means that the bites occurred on the streets and the animal and its owner were never located. However, this does not mean that free-ranging dogs account for only a quarter of the bites. In the opinion of Dr. David Berzon, the city's chief veterinarian, over half the bites from the remaining three-quarters, where the dog or the owner was found, occurred when the dogs were free and unattended. Free-ranging dogs, as defined by this study, inflict a majority of the reported bites.

The significance of any frequency data is unclear. It is estimated that only about half the city's bites are reported (Crawford 1964) and the situation is even more uncertain for the rest of the country. Only eight states reported more than 10,000 dogs bites per state to the Center for Disease Control (CDC) in Atlanta in 1971. Such figures do not reflect the actual number of bites, however; in Maryland, Talbot County, for example, does not report dog bites at all. The CDC lists dogs bite as optionally reportable; thus, comparing the patterns seen in Baltimore with other areas becomes tenuous.

Students of urban ecology feel compelled to compare their data with that from New York City. New York had 37,488 reported dog bites in 1971, about 474 per 100,000 people, which is a much lower rate than Baltimore's. Of course, New York is very diverse. Manhattan, with its people and dogs living mostly in large apartment buildings, has relatively few free-ranging animals and a low reported bite rate. Staten Island in New York City, with much more open space and fewer large apartment buildings, has a reported bite rate of 787 per 100,000, which is comparable to Baltimore's rate. Looking at New York City's statistics as a whole can be very misleading since the city consists of such contrasting physical areas; indeed, New York City is not a typical model for urban studies. Baltimore, like some of the individual New York City boroughs, is more typical of the urban patterns of the United States with respect to density, open space, and types of housing.

Severity

Parrish et al. (1959) studied 947 dog bites reported during the summer of 1958 in Pittsburgh, Pennsylvania. Two percent had no detectable injury, and this category is probably more common but under-reported. Eighty-eight percent of the bites resulted in lacerations and contusion; 9% required one to ten sutures, and one percent required ten or more sutures. Legs were bitten in 39% of these cases; arms in 37%, and the head, face, and neck in 16%.

Dogs killed a Prince George's County (Maryland) girl in 1966 and two boys in a Virginia suburb in 1967 (*Washington Post* articles of the period). In 1970 I interviewed a 6-

year-old boy who required suturing over 90% of his body from an attack by four dogs (see p. 48). The psychological effects on a young victim of dog bites (and on his parents) should not be minimized, regardless of the severity of the injury.

Victims

In Baltimore, 60% of those bitten are under age 15, who constitute less than 30% of the population (D. Berzon et al. 1972). Chi-squared analysis shows this discrepancy to be overwhelmingly significant. Parrish et al. (1959) in Pittsburgh and Brobst, Parrish, and Clack (1959) in Allegheny County (Pennsylvania) present findings very similar to those in Baltimore. Ages five through nine are the highest risk group and males are victims twice as frequently as females at all ages (Parrish et al. 1959). The race of the victim becomes a factor only in the group 20 through 49 years of age. The increase in black victims in this group is probably associated with the higher percentage of blacks in high risk occupations, such as service personnel who walk the streets (Parrish et al. 1959).

Breed, Sex, and Age of the Dogs Involved

In Baltimore, mongrels account for nearly half the bites, possibly because people are less likely to supervise them on the streets. German shepherds account for 64% of the bites from purebreds, even though they constitute only 29% of the purebred population (Berzon 1971). (In 1970, German shepherd sales in the United States were booming.) The higher bite rate with German shepherds was also found in the Pennsylvania studies (Parrish et al. 1959, and Brobst, Parrish and Clack 1959) previously cited. These studies also report that female dogs showed a higher bite rate than males, though more people owned males. Biting was not related to estrous, though the packs that form around an estrous female have not been specifically studied. Younger animals are more bite prone than older dogs; dogs six to eleven months of age are the highest risk group; and I believe over half of Baltimore's free-ranging dog population is under two years of age.

Reasons for Biting

From the opinions of dog owners and of victims, but mostly of uninvolved witnesses, Parrish et al. (1959) found that bites were victim-provoked, play-provoked, or apparently unprovoked with equal frequencies.

In Baltimore, the bite rate doubles during the summer. Figure 7 shows the sharp increase in "10-day" dogs arriving at the pound during the summer months. Parrish et al. note that most winter bites occur on weekends but that this daily variation disappears during the summer. One apparent reason for the increased number of bites during some periods is the increased chance of contact between children and dogs at these times.

Most bites occur in the vicinity of the dog owner's home, which indicates a possible territorial component. The loose pet may very well be a more serious threat to health than the ownerless stray.

Cyclists are often chased by dogs (Eli Freedman, editor of Cyclone Magazine, personal communication). Movement away from the dog may sometimes encourage a dog to bite and may be a factor in these particular dog bites.

In August 1970 a six-year-old boy was attacked in south Baltimore by four dogs. He was on a route near his home that he took almost every morning. He passed an open fence and the resident's dog, a mixed breed (mostly German shepherd), started after him. He realized this and ran. Three other dogs joined the chase and pulled him out of a tree as he tried to escape. The dogs had to be beaten off by two truck drivers. The boy was very nearly killed. He had not entered private property, did not make eye contact with the

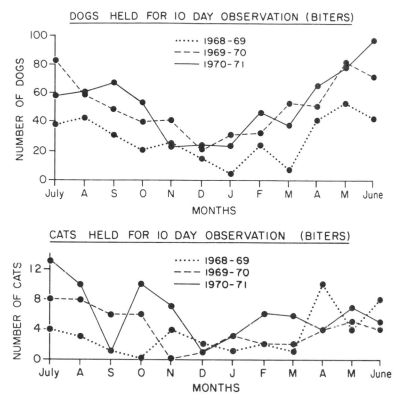

Fig. 7. Dogs and cats held at the Animal Shelter for 10-day observation after biting human beings. Monthly totals are plotted for three years.

dogs (another factor that sometimes encourages attack), and he was acquainted with the dogs prior to the attack. I interviewed residents of the area with the boy's attorney and learned that the initiating dog had a reputation for chasing and biting; it was a watchdog. The other dogs had no such reputation. I observed the four dogs, all mongrels, at the Animal Shelter and they appeared friendly, but the dogs were gassed before more detailed studies were undertaken. This incident exemplifies the role of dog territory, victim movement, and the potential for a socially-facilitated attack. Every parameter of this attack put the boy in the highest risk category—but that still does not explain why the first dog attacked.

Solutions

Enforcement of a law that all dogs must be on leashes would prevent most dog bites. Fear of crime and criminals in urban areas has brought about new interest in "one of the oldest forms of protection: guards dogs trained to attack savagely" (Time 1971); but attack-trained dogs are not suitable house dogs and they should not be kept as pets; to do so invites tragedy.

Burglars fear a dog's bark more than its bite. The primary function of guard dogs should be to warn, not to attack. (See MacInnes 1949 and Caras 1971.) Using dogs as warning systems rather than as weapons is safer, though it does sometimes give rise to a noise problem, to be discussed below.

Bite-prone dogs exist and records should be kept on biters. Permanently marking a biter after the first offense would facilitate record keeping and prevent fraud. More than two bites should not be tolerated.

Parents should be advised of basic precautions which should include not mixing young children and young dogs, discouraging teasing, and not expecting young children to care for a dog. Children should learn not to pet strange dogs and not to try to stop dog fights. Every urban child should be so instructed.

There should be more research on why dogs bite and what one can do to prevent a bite. Herrero (1970) found that not running from grizzly bears may be advisable, and the same may prove true in the case of dogs. I found that holding my ground and feigning to throw an object served me well on various occasions when facing aggressive dogs.

Attacks on other animals are part of the free-ranging dog bite problem. Cities all over the world report attacks on zoo animals. Baltimore lost 49 animals in one night in 1967. Free-ranging dogs, often from cities, kill deer and live-stock throughout the country. Smith (1966) lists the dog only second to fire as the major wildlife problem in Appalachia. He blames public apathy, since the dog is the "sacred cow" of Appalachia, which is perhaps true of much of the nation.

DOGS AND RATS

Fear of rate bites appears to be more widespread in Baltimore than fear of dog bites, even though there were only 32 rat bites in 1970 and 54 in 1971 (compared with 6,023 and 6,809 dog bites during these same two years). Though there have been few diseases directly attributable to rats in Baltimore recently, the mere knowledge of rats in an area is disturbing to residents. Negative feeling for rats, as might be expected, was routinely expressed in interviews and in Housing and Community Development reports.

The relationship of the dog with the brown rat, *Rattus norvegicus*, in an urban setting is an interesting one. Dogs slow down rat eradication crews as they make their rounds, and I have observed people refuse to accept rat poison for fear it would hurt their dog. Rats use the food and water left in yards for pet dogs and rats often burrow under and use dog houses. As free-ranging dogs rummage through garbage they create a poor appearance for the neighborhood, lower trash collection efficiency, and also provide easily acces-sible food for roaches and rats.

In addition to rats' eating garbage made available to them by dogs, they also use dog feces for food, according to residents of rat-infested neighborhoods in Baltimore, an ob-servation confirmed by Charles A. Carroll, the Chief of Baltimore's Rat Eradication Program. I visited one neighbor-hood in the Stony Run-Hamden area of Baltimore where a notable increase in rats had been reported (see Flanery

1971). The "run" was a surface water runoff that backed up during a storm and deposited dog feces in copious quantities along its edge in a park area. This apparently contributed to the increase in the local rat population.

In Baltimore, a landlord is required to remove dog feces from his premises daily if he is served with a rat violation notice (Baltimore City Code, Sec. 902). (Alan Ternes, an urban geographer at Columbia University in New York, has observed pigeons feeding on dog feces, an interesting observation with possible epidemiological implications for all urban wildlife.) Carnivores normally assimilate 30 to 50% of the food they eat (though assimilation of as much as 75% is sometimes possible) (Phillipson 1966). Dogs eating the mixed diet found in garbage probably produce feces that include much that is assimilable by the brown rat.

Another aspect of the ecological relationship between dog and rat has to do with dog-cat interactions. I have observed dogs chase away cats who were stalking rats. The dogs themselves made no attempt to catch rats, and ignored them as they both fed on garbage. In these instances the rats appeared to have no fear of dogs. Smythe (1970) observed a similar interaction in Panama where, if food was plentiful,

Two rats search for food in Baltimore alley. Garbage that is not in covered cans and garbage spilled from cans that have been overturned by dogs make food easily available for rats.

coatis (*Nasua narica*, a carnivore) fed near agoutis (*Dasyprocta punctata*, a rodent). Only when food was scarce would a predator-prey relationship develop—and food is almost always available in inner city alleys.

In addition to dogs aiding rats in several ways, rats also aid dogs. Rats create a social problem which potentially diverts manpower and funds away from dog control. Baltimore spent about $509,842 of its own money for sanitation related to rat control, and $623,310 of federal money on rat control and eradication in 1971 (G. Schucker, Assistant to the Commissioner of Health, Baltimore, personal communication). For this same year the city spent only $237,687 for all dog control functions, with no federal assistance. Dogs and rats obviously enjoy an urban style symbiotic relationship.

Baltimore, like many cities in the United States, is contemplating use of paper and plastic bags for trash instead of noisy, heavy, expensive metal garbage cans. Free-ranging dogs make this alternative less acceptable though further study is indicated.

FECES AND URINE

In 1970 there began to appear articles in the popular press questioning the role of the dog in big cities. "Do cities really need dogs?" (*Time* 1970), "New York: a city going to the dogs" (Berman 1970), "Is Washington really going to the dogs?" (McCarthy 1971), and others appearing in such philosophically dichotomous newspapers as the *Wall Street Journal*: "Awash in excrement, New York fights back against 500,000 dogs" (Kramer 1971), and the *Village Voice:* "One kind of crap you don't have to take" (Whelton 1971). All emphasize one problem—dog feces. (The Washington, D.C., article was immediately followed, in the same issue, by the article "What about the little fella?" [Wool 1971] which is a rebuttal by the editor saying basically that while we don't deny the facts, we love dogs anyway.) The *Wall Street Journal's* article appeared in the center of page one. These and other articles appearing in newspapers around the country were concerned with two problems, the quantity of dog feces in cities and worm infestation in children from fecal contamination of soil. (See also the section below "Diseases Associated with Dogs" beginning on p. 59.)

I was present at a meeting of "Children Before Dogs," a group of citizens organized by consumer advocate Fran Lee, when the police had to be called in to end the fighting between pet owners and others in the audience. It was sad to see people yelling, fighting, and at one point even throwing dog feces at each other. Dog feces were blamed for killing both the "Maxie" style skirts and children.

Quantity of Dog Feces and Urine

New York's Environmental Protection Administration estimates that 4.5 to 18 million kg (5,000 to 20,000 tons) of feces are deposited in the city yearly by its 500,000 dogs. The Bureau of Preventable Diseases estimates a mean fecal output of 0.34 kg per day per dog (0.75 lb per day per dog) based on 482,829 large dogs. New York's upper estimate is three times below what it would be if the population was composed entirely of large dogs. Assuming Baltimore has one-fifth as many dogs as New York, the city would receive some 1.0 to 3.6 million kg (1,000 to 4,000 tons) of feces annually.

Feces usually disappear within a week, but they can remain on the ground for over a month. The daily short term insult to the environment is in the order of 2,700 to 10,000 kg (3 to 11 tons) of feces, if we assume a population of 100,000 dogs.

The same report estimates that the New York dog population deposits 2.3 to 4.0 million liters (600,500 to 1,000,000 gallons) of urine per year. Dogs excrete from 20 to 100 ml of urine per kg body weight per day (Altman 1961). Assuming that the average dog weighs 12 kg (26.4 lbs.) and excretes 60 ml of urine per kg body weight per day, the average urine excretion per dog is 720 ml per day (0.19 gallon). New York's estimate, then, is far too low. This average output in Baltimore would mean 71,000 liters (18,720 gallons) per day of urine.

The actual volume of urine, like feces, varies with diet, fluid intake, climate, and activity. Puppies and younger dogs secrete proportionally larger volumes. The odor of normal urine is due to volatile organic acids (Bloom 1960). While much of the fluid probably evaporates, many of the constituents remain behind. Altman (1961) and Bloom (1960) list the major constituents of dog urine.

Such large quantities of feces and urine have many implications involving the spread of disease, environmental damage, and insult to human senses. The real public health importance has not been clearly determined, and many of the implications are not well understood.

Feces and the Pedestrian

The greatest objections to feces on the streets are to their appearance and odor. People conspicuously avoid direct contact. Various laws prohibiting fecal deposition in the streets (to be discussed later), including the Baltimore City Council's recent curb law (which was vetoed) mostly appear to be in response to esthetic rather than health motives. A law in Nutley (New Jersey), which requires a dog owner to clean up after his pet, was upheld and the judge cited medical evidence regarding fecal dangers. Feces are a form of litter, but a form which by tradition has been exempt from anti-litter enforcement. Public attitude is now changing, possibly encouraged by the new environmental concern sweeping the nation.

Feces and Flies

". . . the truest and simplest way of attacking the fly
problem is to prevent them from breeding, by the treatment
or abolition of all places in which they can breed. To permit
them to breed undisturbed and in countless numbers, and
to devote all our energy to the problem of keeping them out
of our dwellings, or to destroying them after they have once
entered in spite of all obstacles seems the wrong way to go
about it" (Howard 1911). This raises the question of just
what are the breeding places of flies. A survey in Savannah,
Georgia (pop. 130,000) showed that approximately 60% of
all garbage cans actively produced flies and a single dog
fecal deposit produced from 1 to 588 (mean = 144) flies.
After deposition of eggs, burial of the feces in soil as deep
as 452 mm (18 inches) did not affect fly emergence. In residential areas, dog feces ranked next to garbage cans in fly pro-
duction. The percentage of dog stools breeding flies was
higher in better neighborhoods and lower in tenement dis-
tricts (Quarterman, Baker, and Jensen 1949). Feces probably
produce a greater proportion of flies in better neighborhoods
because there is less open garbage. Dogs make garbage available in poorer areas by their rummaging.

The breeding of flies in dog feces is of potential public
health significance because dogs are a frequent host for
enteric organisms such as *Salmonella* of several species
(Wolff, Henderson, and McCallum 1948), and "flies breeding in or feeding upon dog feces might well be considered
as potential sources of *Salmonella* infection in man"
(Quarterman et al. 1949).

Overfertilization of the Terrestial Environment

Fecal overfertilization in the form of agriculturally-
applied fertilizer is well established in rural areas; a special
case takes place in the city where feces deposition results in

the proliferation of pest species like flies, roaches, and rats. Rats and flies have been previously discussed; roaches, often more or less tolerated, are also associated with various human diseases (Sinton 1970).

Tree Kill

Pivone (1969) reports that dog cankers, from direct applications of urine from urinating dogs, kills the bark on trees. The soil associated with such trees contains 900 ppm of soluble salts, several times the maximum tolerance. Baltimore forester Calvin Buikema and I were unable to draw any conclusions from analyses of soil samples around dying trees, because the heavy salting of Baltimore streets in wintertime confused our analyses.) Trees are instrumental in controlling noise and air pollution in the city (Lanphear 1970), as well as in moderating excessive summer heat, and therefore are more of a necessity than a luxury. Anything that inhibits their successful growth must be considered a serious pollutant.

Eutrophy of the Marine Environment

The city is an open ecosystem and its wastes are not usually recycled; instead, they are released to neighboring areas. In Baltimore, storm water runoff is separate from the sanitary system and it drains directly, untreated, into the harbor. Water in Baltimore's harbor shows alarmingly high numbers of coliform bacteria where stormdrains flow from areas in which there is no record of sewage entering the drains. These coliform densities indicate fecal contamination by warm-blooded animals. Though rats, horses, and even humans are possible sources, the dog probably makes the most significant contribution (Wm. Sloan, personal communication). This contaminated runoff will make water contact sports impossible in the harbor area which is now undergoing development. Officials of cities faced with the decision to separate a joint sewage system, which often seems to be indicated as a city grows, should consider the problems of unsanitary storm water carefully before undertaking the tremendous investment required (Geyer and Katz 1965). This aspect of municipal sewage is rapidly becoming a major problem in growing urban areas.

Possible Solutions to the Feces Problem

Keeping dogs free of worms, keeping children away from where dogs defecate, turning the soil and discouraging pica will all help alleviate the public health problems (see below) that can arise from dog feces. Other alternatives directed at lessening the impact of feces should be considered.

"In well-organized communities popular sentiment in favor of further limitation of the freedom of dogs, even those walked on a leash, probably is ready for public expression. It is not now a question of whether promiscuous defecation is a health hazard. The real question is whether a way can be found to discuss this public health problem openly and reach agreement on acceptable control measures" (Beaver 1956).

The first step in the evolution of laws to get feces off public property is at least to get walked-dog excreta off the sidewalks and into the street or gutter. Baltimore has finally joined other cities by trying to adopt a "curb law" (Ordinance 881) introduced in the City Council in November 1970 (but defeated). Such a law, if enforced, would spare some trees from fecal damage, though owners would presumably allow their dogs to urinate in the usual places. Table 1 shows where people walk their dogs; only 18.2% were observed using the street. The curb law would not help solve the sewage runoff problem, of course.

The next step would be the total ban of fecal contamination in public property—the so-called "scoop law." The first such law in the United States was enacted in February 1971 in Nutley, New Jersey, a town of 23,000 people and 2,000 dogs. Basically, the dog owner must retrieve and dispose of feces deposited on public property. Since then several towns on Long Island, N.Y., have passed similar legislation, and cities all over the country are considering the possibility of following Nutley's example.

"Doggie" septic tanks (e.g., Huron Products Co., Bellevue, Ore.) are available for those with private yards for their dogs.

Separate dog areas in parks are a possibility for cities with more than ample park land (if such exist). Fecal retrieval or in-house toileting appear to be the only alternative for the inner city, but for health reasons the job of cleaning up after a dog that uses indoor areas should not be given to young children or pregnant women.

Obviously the laws mentioned here can control only those dogs that never run free. Control of free-ranging dogs will be vital if a city is really serious about curbing fecal contamination.

DISEASES ASSOCIATED WITH DOGS

Visceral Larva Migrans

Of all the diseases associated with dog feces, visceral larva migrans (VLM) is rapidly becoming the best documented in the medical literature. VLM results from the invasion and migration through human viscera of nematode larvae normally found in animals (Dorman and Van Ostrand 1958); it was first described by Beaver et al. (1952). "Why a parasite measuring 400 microns in length and 20 microns in width escaped detection for so many years as a cause of human illness is a puzzling and unanswered question" (Zinkham 1968).

Natural History. VLM is caused most often by the ingestion of the eggs of the nematode, *Toxocara canis,* a parasite of many canids including *Canis lupus, C. dingo, C. aureus, Vulpes vulpes,* and *V. fulva,* as well as *C. familiaris.* It is also reported in *Crocuta crocuta,* the spotted hyena (Sprent 1958). Sprent points out that this wide diversity of hosts gives some indication of its adaptibility. The mode of infection of these different hosts probably includes cannibalism, carrion eating, predation, ingestion of contaminated food, coprophagy, and intrauterine migration. This last mode has been well established in dogs; puppies are often born infected (Yutuc 1949; Fernando 1968). Indeed, migration of the second-stage larva into the liver of the foetus is probably an adaptation to the nonpredatory habits of the dog (Sprent 1958), and may be one reason that similar migration is observed in human infection. Beaver (1959), Warren (1969), Sprent (1958), and Webster (1956) have described both the life cycle in dogs and the abortive cycle observed in man. The eggs hatch in the intestines and the larva of several growth stages migrate into the lungs and up the trachea until the dog coughs and swallows the larva. Development proceeds to the adult stage in the small intestine, where worms mate and fertile ova are passed in the feces, which can infect humans and other animals. Dogs sometimes also shed adult worms which look like thin tan-colored strands that are pointed at both ends. Male worms are hooked at the posterior end. Young hosts, be they children or dogs, are more susceptible than adults. Infection can be established in puppies over six months of age with large doses of ova (Webster 1956), and superinfected puppies that were naturally infected develop a self cure (Fernando 1968). Whereas resistance to infection increases with age, pregnant females often shed ova and give birth to infected young, even if they have appeared to be free of worms, as though the hormonal change of gestation releases larva that have previously been held dormant in the female's system. Basically, then, the mode of infection for dogs is transplacental or by contact with contaminated feces or soil. Such contact is very much part of canine behavior.

Other nematodes to be implicated in VLM include *Toxocara cati, T. leonina,* and *Ancylostoma braziliense* from domestic cats (Ehrenford 1957; Sprent 1956) and *Ancylostoma caninum* in dogs (Beaver 1959). The *Ancylostomas* are hookworms previously thought to be associated only with creeping eruptions or cutaneous larva migrans in man, but now there is evidence that they too may migrate internally. *Anclyostoma* is more common in adult dogs of both sexes than in puppies (Beaver 1959).

Frequency of Toxocara *in Dogs.* No frequency study for *Toxocara* has been undertaken in Baltimore, though most veterinarians believe it to be extremely common, especially in puppies. In Washington, D.C., Wright (1930) reported 33.3% infection in 150 dogs. Ehrenford (1957) found a *Toxocara* incidence in 1,324 dogs of 34.2% in males and 12.7% in females, for immature dogs, and 31.2% in males and 4.9% in females for mature animals in the Ohio River drainage basin. He noted that males show an increase in infection during the winter months whereas females are more uniformly infected. Age resistance develops in females by 3 to 6 months, but resistance in males is much lower. About 1.0% of the cats in Ehrenford's study had *T. cati* or *T. leonina.* Vaughn and Jordon (1960) sampled dog stools from different socioeconomic neighborhoods in New Orleans as well as those in veterinary clinics and found only slight differences between infection in dogs confined to the house except for exercise (48% of 32) and those allowed yard or neighborhood freedom (58% of 147). Frequency in well-cared-for dogs is relatively lower. Beaver (1959) sampled 171 fresh dog stools collected along the sidewalks in front of the houses of "perhaps the most sanitation-minded, hygiene-conscious, and economically most favored families in the city" (New Orleans), and 7% contained *T. canis* eggs; hookworm eggs were found in 51%; and *Trichuris* in 25%. Almost all of these stools were judged to have come from adult dogs. The findings are "disturbingly high" (Beaver 1959). Dorman and Van Ostand (1958) found a surprisingly low incidence of *Toxocara canis* (1.6%) and *Ancylostoma caninum* (6.8%) in the New York City area from 500 stools, but they sampled only during the summer and did not distinguish age or sex. They suggested that the potential health hazard was not as great as anticipated, but they did not question why their results were so much lower than all other studies.

The eggs of these parasites are extremely persistent and can survive many months under a variety of environmental conditions (Beaver 1956; R. Lennox, personal communication). Relatively few eggs added daily to the soil tend to maintain large numbers of infective stages in the surface layer (Vaughn and Jordon 1960). Eggs require only a little moisture (like dew) and a slight amount of oxygen to embryonate and become infective.

Mode of infection in humans. Humans, usually children, ingest infective eggs after handling puppies, while breathing dusty air where fecal material has dried, or while playing in or eating dirt where eggs have accumulated. Geophagy (dirt eating) or pica is very common among children. Dickens and Ford (1942) observed geophagy in 26% of the boys and 25% of the girls of 207 third graders is Mississippi. They point out that the incidence is probably higher than average because the children came from poor families. The implication was that they suffered from some nutrient deficiency neutralized by the consumed clay or dirt. However, Vermeer (1971 and personal communication) has been studying extensive geophagy in Ghana and has little evidence that there is any nutrient value in the clay. Cooper (1957) in Baltimore found that 53.3% of the black and 44.7% of the white children ($N = 784$) sampled at a health center ate dirt alone or with plaster. Pica usually develops at about 2 years of age and disappears at 4 to 5 years and is generally associated with lower than average IQ and feeding problems.

Whether geophagy is a response to a dietary need or just a pattern of childhood is not clear, but in any event it sets the stage for ingestion of nematode ova. In Baltimore, where children and dogs compete for the dirt under trees and in small parks, loose dogs pose a special problem. It should also be remembered that as eggs accumulate they may be transferred by rain-drop splash, water currents, wind, insects, and soiled shoes and clothing, so eggs and larvae in unsuspected sites are possible. Damaging infection in children who have had no known contact with a pet has occured (Beaver 1956; Vaughn and Jordon 1960; and Zinkham 1968). Enclosed yards shared by children and dogs are ideal sites for infection.

Human infection. Two ideas should be remembered before considering the frequency and symptomology of VLM. First inability of a parasite to complete its life cycle because it is in the wrong host should not be equated with a lack of infectivity; and second, it is misleading to discuss prevalence of a disease for which there is no specific diagnostic test. The references cited in this chapter include over 300 cases of VLM, but the actual frequency in man is unknown, and even a gross estimate is not possible at this time.

Though many nematode parasites are specific to a particular host, aberrant parasitism, as with VLM, has been observed often and is important in the evolution of host-parasite relationships. Webb (1965) pointed out there are some 130–150 major and 80–90 minor public health diseases common to man and animals. Diseases shared by man and domestic animals are long standing and have usually evolved to benign forms. Cross invaders are also seen, e.g., measles from distemper and smallpox from cowpox. Though reinfection back to animals is possible with some diseases, VLM is a dead end for *Toxocara*, since the larvae fail to mature in man. Adult worms are only passed if the child eats the adult worm or a very late larval stage.

Several VLM cases have been reported in the literature (Brown 1970; Heiner 1956; Huntley, Costas, and Lyerly 1965; Milburn and Ernst 1953; Snyder 1961; Wilder 1950;

Wilkenson and Welch 1971; Wright and Gold 1946; and
Zinkham 1968). Major symptoms of systemic infection include hepatomegaly, splenomegaly, convulsion, fever, wheez-
ing, anemia, and a marked eosinophilia (up to 90%). The
patients are usually children under six and often, but not
always, have a history of pica. Actual known contact with
dogs did not appear significant. A special form of VLM
occurs when the larvae invade the eye. Wilder (1950) examined 46 eyes that were enucleated for suspected retino-
blastomas and found 26 contained either nematode larva or
their residual hyaline capsules. Zinkham (1968), Brown
(1970), and Wilkinson and Welch (1971) all discuss ocular
involvement; the latter includes 13 new cases found at The
Johns Hopkins Hospital in 1971; one case involved both
eyes. In 1972 there were several new cases (R. Welch, personal
communication). In the last 10 years the ages of patients
hospitalized at Johns Hopkins for *Toxocara* infection has
ranged from 2 to 62 years, and males have significantly out-
numbered females. There are two reasons why the occular
form deserves special attention; (i) blindness or even partial
blindness at a young age is a great personal and social tragedy,
and (ii) ocular involvement permits a specific diagnosis.

All too often VLM is confused with other childhood
diseases or is undiagnosed, since the larvae are not observed
(as they can be in the eye). The best photographs of larval
migration appear in Rubin et al. (1967). Biopsy for the larvae
is unrealistic. There is not yet any specific skin test that can
distinguish *T. canis* from any other nematode, such as the
human nematode *Ascaris lumbricoides*. It is interesting to
note that ocular involvement is not usually associated with
pica (Zinkham 1968), which suggests the possibility of a
direct mode of entry into the eye.

VLM is so new and its implications so alarming that a
recent case was described by a local tabloid (Tripp, 1971).
The 4-year-old child mentioned, who lost sight in one eye,
was seen at Hopkins hospital and the story was verified. The
more conservative newspapers did not cover the story, pos-

sibly because people are not comfortable with the idea that the dog, pet and friend, can blind children. An organization, Children Before Dogs, has been formed in New York to educate people about possible dangers of pet ownership, and its director, Fran Lee, is subject to severe harassment when interviewed on television or in the newspapers (Nobile 1971 and F. Lee, personal communication). Dog owners often show a surprising resistance to learning anything negative about dogs, even when their own children may be involved.

There is a need for a method for specific diagnosis of VLM. Hogarth-Scott, Johansson, and Bennich (1969) and Schiller (1967) have shown that there are significant changes in certain antibody levels in response to *Toxocara* that may permit accurate diagnosis and make screening for true prevalence a possibility. A well-coordinated epidemiological survey of children, soil and dogs might make it possible to judge the significance of the problem (Schiller, personal communication). Goss and Rebrassier (1922) outline a technique for examining dog feces for parasite infection.

Other Diseases Associated with Dogs

Zoonoses associated with dogs sometimes involve fecal contact, as discussed above, but other modes of transmission are common. Hull (1963) lists some 65 diseases that have been spread from dog to man, including diseases from viruses, Rickettsia, bacteria, fungi, protozoa, nematoda, cestoda, and arthropoda. "Among human infections besides measles and mumps that may be acquired by the dog and passed back to man, are the human type of tuberculosis, diphtheria, and scarlet fever. Dogs should not be allowed close contact therefore, with persons suffering from those diseases " (Hull 1963, p. 895).

Dogs harboring and transmitting tuberculosis (*Mycobacterium bovis* and *M. tuberculosis*) do not necessarily show any symptoms and are especially dangerous to children because of the potential for very close contact during frequent fondling and play. In one study, the owners of 14 tuberculous dogs underwent x-ray examination, which revealed that nine (over half) of the individuals needed to be treated for tuberculosis (Hawthorne et al. 1957). In a later study, evidence of tuberculosis, active at a relevant time, was found in 41 of 354 people (11.8%) who had contact with 31 dogs that died of tuberculosis (Hawthorne and Lauder 1962). Apparently dogs can serve as a reservoir for tuberculosis, and the infection can be passed either from man to dog or from dog to man. The authors advocate the reporting of tuberculous animals to public health authorities as is done with human cases.

Histoplasmosis (caused by *Histoplasma capsulatum*) also can be caught from dogs, who pick up the fungus from the soil (Hull 1963; Bisseru 1967). The fungus has been cultured from suppurating cutaneous lesions of dogs, from dog sputum, and from the dog tick, *Dermacentor variabilis* (Bisseru 1967).

Arthropod-vectored diseases from dogs are also known. For example, the dog heartworm (*Dirofilaria immitis*), a mosquito-borne parasite, has been reported in man (Beaver and Orihel 1965; Beskin, Colvin, and Beaver 1966; Tuazon, Firestone, and Blaustein 1967).

Dogs probably serve as reservoirs for various rickettsia that infect man. Even though they do not usually show signs of disease, when dogs are infected with ticks carrying rickettsia, they commonly develop antibodies against these microorganisms. Ticks often do carry rickettsial diseases, and they are frequent dog ectoparasites; thus, their transfer to man is not only annoying, but potentially hazardous. Between 1931 and 1950, tick-borne typhus (Rocky Mountain spotted fever) was reported from all sections of Maryland except the three westernmost counties (Price 1954). In 1970 Maryland had the third highest number of cases in the United States, with nearby Virginia and North Carolina being first and second, respectively (Peters 1971). In 1971 Maryland had 31 of the country's 404 cases. The American dog tick, *Dermacentor variabilis,* which parasitizes small mammals in sylvan areas is the primary vector of tick-borne typhus. This tick has been recovered occasionally from Baltimore dogs, especially those that run through woodlots; the brown tick, *Rhipicephalus sanquiueus,* a possible vector, is extremely common on stray dogs.

One of the most serious diseases popularly (and correctly) thought to be associated with dogs is the virus disease, rabies. The earliest recorded epidemics of rabies among urban dogs occurred in Europe and in America (Virginia and North Carolina) in the 1700's, and such epidemics have been of concern to health authorities ever since. All species of warm-blooded animals are susceptible to rabies, but in urban areas when man is infected it is most commonly by the bite of a rabid dog.

In Baltimore there has not been a recorded case of dog rabies for 25 years; however, in 1971, 676 rabid animals (including 82 dogs and 28 cats) were reported within 300 miles of the city. Nearby Virginia and West Virginia had 200 of the cases, including 36 dogs and 19 cats. In 1972, several rabid bats occurred in Maryland and within the city of Baltimore (D. Berzon, personal communication). Baltimore's one rabid bat was brought into the house by the family cat, which exemplifies a very feasable mode of rabies transmission to man. Rabid cats are a threat to dogs and man. Rabies is increasing in frequency in the red fox around the country. City forester Calvin Buikema and I have seen this species well within Baltimore's city limits.

Feces and Urine Associated with Other Diseases. "Dogs are assuming an increasing importance in the epidemiology of leptospirosis, especially the disease due to *Leptospira canicola* and *L. icterhaemorrhagiae*" (Hull 1963). Hirschberg, Maddry, and Hines (1956) report that leptospirosis is on the increase, mostly in children, and that 15 to 18 dogs sampled at random were positive for *L. canicola.* The bacteria are passed in the urine to soil.

Brucellosis or undulant fever is caused by a variety of

species of *Brucella* from direct contact or from contamination with feces and urine. The disease, on the increase as new varieties of the bacteria appear (Bisseru 1967; Hoag 1970; David Berzon, personal communication), continues as a public health problem, with dogs as potential carriers.

Various species of worms, in addition to those involved in visceral larva migrans, may pass from dog to man. For example, *Trichuris* (whipworm), probably *T. vulpis*, was obtained from the feces of a sick 4-year-old boy whose only animal contact was with the three bird dogs kept in the back yard at his grandparents' farm. When the boy became ill the two dogs that were living were examined and found to be infested with *T. vulpis* (Hall and Sonnenberg 1956). The tapeworms *Dipylidium caninium* and *Echinococcus granulosis* are found in dogs, and human infection acquired from dogs is well established (Faust, Beaver and Jung 1968). In cases of *Echinococcus* hydatid cysts, exposure usually precedes diagnosis by 5 to 20 years.

Hull (1963), Faust et al. (1968), and Bisseru (1967) all list other diseases associated with dog feces and urine, though they are often rare in the U.S., but significant in tropical or underdeveloped countries.

NOISE

"The dog barking at you from behind his master's fence acts from a motive indistinguishable from that of his master when the fence was built" (Ardrey 1967, p. 5).

With 30 to 50% of families owning dogs, and with several families per row house, nearly every back yard bordering the alleys of Baltimore contains a captive dog. These penned pets are often provoked into barking by free-ranging dogs, and of course barking begets barking so that long bouts of chain-reaction barking may travel down an alley. Thus, while dogs loose on the streets seldom exhibit territorial barking, nevertheless their movements are a source of noise pollution in the city. With urban crime very much in the news media, people tend to keep larger dogs with louder and deeper vocalizations and, indeed, these dogs' barking abilities are often encouraged in the hopes they will serve some warning function.

Barking, especially at night, is one of the objections to dogs expressed in my interviews with residents. Many suburban housewives have written to me to tell me of the noise problem from dogs in their particular communities; on Long Island many towns now include legal control over barking animals as they update their dog ordinances.

Noise intensity (loudness) is not the only parameter of barking that interests those concerned with public health. Glass and Singer (1971) have shown that exposure to noise impairs subsequent tolerance for frustration as well as the quality of task performance; the degree of impairment is appreciably worse if the noise is unpredictable and uncontrollable. Post-exposure behavioral deficits persist even if the subject apparently "adapts" to the physiological effects of the exposure. Roth, Kramer, and Trinder (1971), investigating the effects of noise exposure during sleep on post-sleep behavior, found that sleep disruption was age-related. Subjects 50 to 70 years old were disturbed more by the noise than younger subjects and suffered greater impairment of memory tasks and cognitive abilities. The older groups also suffered impairment in handling human relations following a night with six to ten noise presentations, even though these presentations were not necessarily loud enough to cause full awakening.

In a city filled with unpredictable and uncontrollable noises, dog barking is yet another potential for lowering the quality of life for the urban dweller.

CHAPTER FOUR

Recommendations for Urban Dog Control

Baltimore attempts to control free-ranging dog populations in two ways. First, there is a leash law (which is rarely enforced) that pet dogs may not be on public property unless they are restrained by a leash no longer than six feet or are muzzled. Second, the Municipal Animal Shelter retrieves strays from the streets whether or not they are licensed. Dogs on private property, even lawns and steps, lactating females, and those under six months, may not be captured.

Implementation of the following suggestions might improve stray dog control. First, muzzled dogs should not be allowed to run free. They pose as much of a traffic hazard and contribute as much to fecal pollution as any dog does; in addition, muzzling leaves a dog virtually defenseless and is unfair, even dangerous, to a free-ranging dog. Second, the leash law should be strictly enforced and heavier penalties imposed. Presently, guilty owners pay only $1.00 per day for the first four days, then 50¢ per day up to seven days for housing at the shelter. If the dog is unlicensed, an additional $5.00 fee is required. These rates are lower than those in other parts of the state.

After observing the Animal Shelter in operation and collating the ideas of the personnel I suggest the following:

Present emergency service operates during usual business hours to meet the needs of those requiring house service. I recommend funds be made available for another shift, from 0600 to 1200 hours. This patrol would have the advantages of being free to catch strays during the dogs' morning activity period (see Fig. 2) and still be on the streets to answer house calls after the activity period ends, usually by 0830 hours. With early morning patrols there is a possibility of collecting more ownerless strays and not just loose pets. Removing nuisance animals, not just pets, would enhance the image of the shelter which would increase its efficiency by lessening harassment; and it would encourage people to use the service more frequently.

Another way to improve the image of the shelter would be to make literature available which should explain the philosophy and practices of dog control. This literature, in the form of pamphlets, should be more than mere public relations; it should be a clearly written informative statement of how dog ownership must be accompanied by social responsibility, together with some of the basic (not exaggerated) public health implications of an ever-growing stray population. Pound crews should disseminate these pamphlets when queried by people. At the moment there is no such literature available and crews cannot take the time to answer the many questions asked, a situation which only leads to misinformation and unnecessary mistrust of municipal functions.

There should be additional patrolling for strays during the summer months and weekends when dog and child activity is greatest, as reflected by the sharp increase in reported dog bites.

The law should be changed to allow pound crews to collect strays from open private property. Indeed, loose dogs on private property are more likely to bite mailmen, service personnel, and passing pedestrians than are other free-ranging dogs. Crews should also be allowed to collect young dogs.

The shelter should experiment with new patterns of operation. At the moment, during full operation there are two trucks, with two men each, for each half of the city. All trucks go on house calls and collect strays en route. It has been suggested that one truck with one worker might handle all the house calls (which require only one person) and that another truck with two aboard handle only stray collecting. The money saved by having one less worker on a shift could be applied to an early morning shift.

Shelter facilities, especially for housing quarantined animals (biters) should be expanded.

Funds for shelter improvement might come from an increased licensing of dogs as a result of using dog wardens; federal financial assistance, as with rat control, might also be feasible.

There is a growing feeling in many cities that tax-supported pet sterilizing programs would alleviate the stray problem. Such a program would be very expensive and take funds away from where they could be of use. If the leash law is enforced there is no need for the public to pay a pet owner's veterinary bills. In fact, there is the danger that a sterilizing program may be misinterpreted as license to let pets run free. Sterile dogs, after all, also disrupt garbage, defecate, and bite. Pet ownership is a privilege, not a right, and privileges need not be state subsidized.

Rabies vaccinations should be required in Baltimore and they should be subsidized in the interests of public health.

A general program of education should advise people about the best kinds of dogs to own, and how to behave when confronted by a free-ranging animal. Such information should be disseminated to the public, and should be included in school curricula along with other aspects of environmental safety.

People should know that working dogs (German shepherds, Doberman pinschers, collies, boxers) and sporting dogs (pointers, setters, retrievers) are involved in more bite incidents than is expected by chance, whereas hounds bite fewer people than expected. Furthermore, female dogs tend to bite more often than males. Several authorities recommend that families with young children (under age six) should not own dogs.

Teaching materials should be prepared—probably audio-visual materials would be most effective—showing children what to do when confronted by an aggressive stray dog. Until more research (for which there is a need) establishes better techniques, the advice not to run, but to shout and feign to throw a missile appears to be generally useful. Both children and adults must be reminded that their dogs should not run free in cities, not only because dogs pose a potential threat to the health and safety of people in cities, but because man's cities are a real threat to the safety of any roaming dog.

Finally, it is time to recognize and to openly discuss the public health problems associated with dogs, along with dogs' virtues and values. The apparent ban on such discussion, as demonstrated in the violent incident mentioned in Chapter Three must end so that urban people can work together rationally to make cities into places where dog and man can live together in health and peace.

Appendix

METHODS FOR ECOLOGICAL PARAMETERS

Origin

Information on the origin of free-ranging dogs was obtained whenever possible from general observations and discussions with local residents. Records from the Municipal Animal Shelter (dog pound) were also analyzed.

Abundance

The systematic survey described next under "Photographic Recapture Method" generated the data that was analyzed by the four methods to be discussed. All these surveys began from 0600 to 0715 and within that range there was no significance to the precise beginning time. Only free-ranging dogs were counted in the surveys.

Photographic Recapture Method (Schnabel). This is a modification of Schnabel's (1938) variation of the Petersen-Lincoln Index using multiple recaptures. Every dog observed within one half block of my car was photographed as I rode the same route for nine consecutive days. (A 105 mm lens with 35 mm black and white film was used.) The individual differences between dogs made it possible to recognize individuals and to determine whether or not a dog had been previously photographed, i.e., "recaptured." Trapping the

74

animal to put on additional markings was never necessary.
By setting each day's captures (photos) next to each other on
a table, I was able to compute recaptures. The formula
employed was:

$$\hat{K} = \frac{\Sigma\,(X_i\,X_m)}{\Sigma\,(X_{i,m}) + 1}$$

where X_i are daily captured totals, $X_{i,m}$ dogs previously photographed (captured), K is the estimator of the total population, and $X_m = X_i - X_{i,m}$ or dogs photographed for the first
time and considered marked or recaptured if photographed
again on subsequent days.

The addition of one to (X_{im}) is Chapman's improvement of the original formula. The formula is directly analogous to Petersen's original formula for just two days of
observations:

$$\hat{K} = \frac{X_1\,X_2}{X_{1,2}}$$

where X_1 and X_2 are the two respective captures and $X_{1,2}$ are
the recaptures. The logic of the method is basically that the
subjects captured the first time are to the whole population
as the numbers captured the second time are to those captured twice. This is the logic of dilution, and was first used
by La Place in 1783 to sample people.

The multiple recapture variation in general is superior
to the two sample method, since capture-recapture ratios are
averaged, thus reducing sample error. One advantage that
photographic recapture has over actual capture is that there
is no possibility of the animal's developing trap shyness or
proness, since he does not know he has been "trapped." (City
dogs are habituated to passing automobiles; they ignored me
and did not even know they were being studied.) Another

advantage is that photographing is faster than checking and rebaiting traps, and a larger area can be sampled. In addition, large-scale capture of dogs for study in Baltimore would not have been possible because of the widespread protective social attitudes regarding dogs. Photos of dogs that were too unclear to permit positive identification were treated as animals who lost their tags, that is, they were counted but not considered as recaptures.

Flyger (1959) estimated squirrel populations by initially trapping the animals in order to add conspicuous markings; but he then relied on subsequent sight recapture. He found that the population estimates based on just sighting the animals were more accurate than those based on actual recapture, becuase of the obvious problems of trap bias. Working with dogs (which are easily distinguishable as individuals) gives one the advantage of eliminating all trapping.

The formula (see Overton 1971) employed for generating the 95% confidence limits for the population estimate, K, when using the Schnabel method was:

$$K_l, K_u = \hat{K}\left(1 \pm \frac{2}{\sqrt{X_{i,m}}}\right)$$

where K_l and K_u are the lower and upper limits of K, respectively (my notation).

The method is best suited when there are more than 50 recaptures and assumes a reasonably accurate approximation to the Poisson distribution. The frequency distribution of observed dog-group sizes superficially approximated a zero-truncated Poisson, but not precisely as judged by goodness-of-fit tests (see "Social Organization" in this appendix). The confidence limits were used when extrapolating the dog population for the whole city.

Darroch's Multiple-Recapture Census Method. Basically Darroch's (1958) model states (using my notation, not Dar-

roch's) that an equation for the maximum likelihood estimates $\widehat{K}$ of K must be one of the roots of

$$\prod_i (K - a_i) = K^{s-1} (K - r)$$

where $a_i =$ the size of the ith sample (which ranged from 11
to 27 dogs per day), $s =$ the total number of samples (9 in the
present study), and

$$r = \sum_\omega u_\omega = \sum_i u_i + \sum_{i<j} u_{i,j} + \ldots + u_{1,2,\ldots 5},$$

or 107 different animals in my study, where u_i is the number
of individuals caught in the ith sample but not otherwise, $u_{i,j}$
the number caught in the ith and j^{th} sample but not otherwise
and similarly $u_{i,j,k}$ etc. and ω denotes the subset $1,2,3,\ldots 5$. Then

$$a_i = \sum_{\omega \supset i} u_\omega$$

where summation is over all subsets ω (samples) which include the integer i.

The derivation of the original formula in Darroch's
paper is too lengthy to be repeated here; the advantage of
using Darroch's estimator is that is utilizes the data from
my observations of 107 different dogs, a parameter not used
in the Schnabel estimator.

The root is found to be the best fit using the Newton-
Raphson method.

There are no published confidence limits associated with
Darroch's estimator.

Hanson's Estimator for unidentified individuals. I employed Hanson's (1968) model by plotting every dog photographed on a map of the one-quarter square mile area for
each day then superimposed a grid of 100 squares (of $1/400$
square mile area) over each day's map in turn. For each day
I recorded the numbers of dogs that were covered by grids
that had not contained dogs on previous days.

Hanson proposed that an animal population be uniformly surveyed by rapid, cursory observations on an area that has been subdivided into equal sample spaces (plots). The counts are incomplete since the observer does not attempt to see all of the animals. During each inspection the total number of observed animals and their plots are noted; such plots are removed from further consideration. If emigration and migration between plots are assumed to cancel, and the population does not change between surveys, this plot removal is analogous to actual removal but has the advantages that it does not interfere with the study population and does not require the labor of catching and removing animals. Hanson derives the formula:

$$\hat{K} = \frac{X_1}{1 - (\sum_{i=2}^{n} X_i / \sum_{i=1}^{n-1} X_i)^{1/2}}$$

where $X_1 =$ the number "removed" on the first survey and $X_i =$ the numbers "removed" during any given survey from the first $(i = 1)$ to the last $(i = n)$ surveys.

Hanson (1968) proposed that the various methods for estimating animal populations by actual removal of animals (Zippen 1958) could be analogously applied by mathematical removal. Trap removal studies use various formulas that estimate the slope of the line generated when the daily removal recorded is plotted against the animals previously removed. This line can be extended to cross the theoretical point on the graph of total removal, i.e., the population that must be present.

I analyzed the data by mathematically removing dogs, then reanalyzed by mathematically removing groups, regardless of size, including groups of one dog. Both methods of analysis were undertaken in the assumption that dogs are not distributed at random but are probably clumped because they are attracted to each other, i.e., because they show pack behavior. The frequency distribution of group sizes will be discussed later under "Social Organization."

Hanson suggested that the formula is most applicable if the probability (P) of seeing any one given animal on a survey is $P_i \geqslant 0.3$, which requires that

$$(\sum_{i=2}^{n} X_i / \sum_{i=1}^{n-1} X_i) \leqslant (0.7)^{1/2} \leqslant (0.84).$$

He explains that the method is biased slightly downward but the bias becomes less as the size of the sample plots is made smaller. The P_i for 1970 and 1971 were individuals = 0.93, groups = 0.91 and individuals = 0.86, groups = 0.72, respectively, indicating that the dog is a good study species for this model.

It should be noted that this method gave results that agreed very closely with those of the two recapture methods previously discussed. Estimates of abundance tend to be validated when several methods, differing conceptually, give comparable results (Hanson 1963).

The data collected for this method were also analyzed using Hanson's (1967) "relation of variance to mean" model, but the daily variance of the number of dogs observed proved too great for this model. Applying the method requires so little additional analysis that future investigators may want to pursue the method if they are also using the Hanson model that has just been discussed. Basically the numbers of dog groups observed in the sample plots are counted, without removal, and the observed mean $(\bar{x})$ and variance (s^2) is applied to the formula: $\hat{K} = \bar{x}^2/(\bar{x} - s^2)$. The derivation of this easily applied formula is given in Hanson (1967) and discussed further by Overton (1971).

Proportion Method. I applied a cursory survey to other one-quarter square mile areas, reasoning that if the original study area yielded an average of 17.7 dogs per run (all runs included) and had a population between 150 and 200 dogs

(using previously described methods) then the average seen
on any new one-quarter square mile plot (of similar topography) should hold a population directly proportional to
17.7/150 for the low estimate and 17.7/200 for the high estimate, i.e., I multiplied the average number of dogs observed
after several runs by 8.47 and 11.29 for low and high estimates, respectively.

Distribution

On two different occasions the whole city was surveyed
by 30 people the first time and 8 the second. Each person was
given a city map on which a specific route was outlined.
Each person drove his route beginning at 0630 and noted
the numbers of dogs and group sizes observed. In effect, this
method is fanning out to "beat the bushes" to locate animals
at one point in time. The data were analyzed by preparing
a composite map.

Activity

Activity periods were determined by following specific
free-ranging dogs for several days. Behaviors, locations, and
times were recorded. In addition, the main study area was
surveyed every hour over a three-day period and the numbers
of humans and dogs were recorded for each hourly survey.
Each of these hourly surveys took about 15 minutes.

Land Use Patterns

Patterns of how dogs use city space (use patterns) were
derived by recording the location of every observed dog
during the 1970 and 1971 population surveys. Additional
information came from informal street interviews and a systematic interview of every head of household at home on one
street in the main study area.

Home Range

Two dogs, which I called "Shaggy" and "Doberman" for convenience, were followed extensively during the summer of 1969. By plotting the outermost points of their range after following the dogs for many days, as well as adding any sightings made during routine checks of the main area, I obtained an estimate of the home range of these two inten- sively-studied dogs.

Food and Water Procurement

General information on how the dogs obtained food and water was derived from field observations and interviews. The effects of trash collection were determined by analyzing the numbers of dogs observed during the population surveys grouped by days of trash collection. The main study area was grouped into two one-eighth square mile plots of differing trash collection patterns.

Shelter

Information about where the dogs found shelter was derived from field observations, from interviews, and from accompanying the city's Housing Authority photographer on his visits to vacant buildings.

Social Organization

Group patterns were analyzed from the data generated by the population abundance surveys.

The morning population surveys showed the distribu- tion of dog groups (Table 2) to resemble superficially a zero- truncated Poisson curve. The zero-truncation is necessary as group size zero is impossible. To test the hypothesis that the observed distribution was no different than the zero-truncated Poisson, theoretically expected group size frequencies were generated using

$$P(k/\lambda) = \lambda^k/(e^\lambda - 1)\,k$$

where $k =$ the frequencies of group sizes 1,2,3,4,5, or more; and λ is the maximum likelihood estimator (J. Cohen 1969; 1971). A. C. Cohen (1960) derives the formula $\bar{x} = \lambda\,(1 - e^{-\lambda})$ which can be used to estimate λ, and he also provides tabled values of λ requiring that only $\bar{x}$ (the mean) be known. The observed group mean was 1.41001, (including solitary animals as groups of one for statistical purposes) from which a λ of 0.7316 can be estimated. The Poisson equation above is then solved five times using $k = 1,2,\ldots 5$ or more, to generate the expected frequency probabilities for each group size. The probabilities are then each multiplied by 377, the number of groups observed, to generate the numbers of each group size expected. For sizes (k) 1,2,...5 or more, these expected frequencies are 255.76, 93.56, 22.81, 4.17, and 0.69, respectively. These expected frequencies can now be compared with the observed frequencies (namely 270, 69, 29, 7, and 2, respectively) using the chi-square goodness-of-fit test, with 3 degrees of freedom (d.f.), as there are five cells but one d.f. is lost as frequencies must sum to 377; another is absorbed when λ was estimated. A chi square of 13.291 is generated, which is far too large to have arisen by chance and the hypothesis that the frequencies observed is no different than a zero-truncated Poisson is rejected. As an additional test, Cohen (1971) suggests a variation of the Poisson variance test for the zero-truncated Poisson, namely, $x^2 = (T - 1)\,s^2/(1 - P_1')\,\bar{x}$ with $T - 1$ degrees of freedom where x^2 is an estimator for chi-square, T is the number of independent observations, $P_1' = \lambda/(e^\lambda - 1)$ is the probability of groups of size one (λ estimated as before), and s^2 and $\bar{x}$ are the sample variance and mean, respectively. Using $T = 377$,

$x^2 = 473.865$, which is also far too large, with 376 degrees of freedom, to accept the hypothesis that dog group frequencies are approximately a 0-truncated Poisson distribution.

As suggested by W. Cocran (personal communication) the daily mean group size for my 28 days of observations was tested using

$$X^2 = \sum_{i=1}^{28} n_i \, (\bar{x}_i - \bar{x})^2 / s^2$$

with 27 degrees of freedom, where $n_i =$ number of groups on day i, and $\bar{x}_i =$ mean size on day i and was found to have a $x^2 = 63.96$ which exceeds that 0.01 level indicating that the daily group size mean fluctuated significantly from day to day. Therefore, even if the group size distribution was Poisson on any given day, the daily variation was so great that it rules out the possibility that the dogs were behaving uniformly (J. Cohen, personal communication).

Mortality

Patterns of mortality were derived by analyzing Animal Shelter records and by estimating the ages of dead dogs brought in from the streets by shelter personnel. Estimations of age were made by using the tooth eruption and wear patterns listed by Archibald (1965) and Siegmund (1967). Age at time of death was then used to develop a life table (Table 4 in the text) as outlined by Deevey (1947).

Accompanying animal shelter and rat eradication crews and interviewing officials of various city agencies were also part of the methods employed. Records from the city's Health Department and from Johns Hopkins Hospital were reviewed for various pertinent statistics.

The ecological data were obtained without interfering with the dogs' normal behavior, except on one occasion when two dogs were live-trapped from the Chapel Gate area using a Thompson trap "baited" with a rag that was soaked with urine from a bitch in estrous. Otherwise, animals were never detained or attracted in any way.

Literature Cited

Ables, E. D. 1969. Home-range studies of red foxes (*Vulpes vulpes*). J. Mamm. 50:108–120.

Acha, R. N. 1969. Algunas consideraciones sobre las condiciones actuales de la rabia en las Americas. Boletin de la Official Sanitaria Panamericana 66:211–217.

Adams, L., and S. D. Davis. 1967. The internal anatomy of home range. J. Mamm. 48:529–536.

Altman, P. L. 1961. Blood and other body fluids. Commission on Biological Handbooks. Bethesda, Maryland: Fed. of Am. Societies for Exper. Biol. 540 pp.

Anderson, R. W., and J. R. Cameron. 1955. Registration without taxation—Denver's approach to rabies control. Am. J. Pub. Health 45:1005–1010.

Archibald, J. 1965. Canine surgery. Santa Barbara, Calif.: Amer. Veterinary Publications, Inc. 1024 pp.

Archibald, W. S., and S. J. Kunitz. 1971. Detection of plaque by testing serums of dogs on the Navajo reservation. HSMHA Health Rep. 86:377–380.

Ardrey, R. 1967. The territorial imperative. New York: Atheum. 390 pp.

Barbehenn, K. 1969. Responses of rodents and shrews to patterns of removal trapping, p. 247–252. *In* D. W. Parrack (ed.). Indian Rodent Sym., Calcutta, India, December 1966. New Delhi: Caxton Press Ltd.

Beaver, P. C. 1956. Visceral larva migrans—a public health problem? Public Health Rep. 71:298–299.

———. 1959. Visceral and cutaneous larva migrans. Public Health Rep. 74:328–332.

Beaver, P. C., and T. C. Oribel. 1965. Human infection with Filariae of animals in the United States. Am. J. Trop. Med. Hyg. 14:1010–1029.

Beaver, P. C., et al. 1952. Chronic eosinophilia due to visceral larva migrans. Report of three cases. Pediatrics 9:7–19.

Beck, A. M. 1971. The life and times of shag, a feral dog in Baltimore. Natural History 80(8):58–65 (October).

Bell, J. F. 1967. Present concepts of the epidemiology of rabies. First Internat. Confer. on Vaccines against Viral & Rickettsial Diseases of Man, PAHO/WHO p. 481–487.

Berman, C 1970. New York: a city going to the dogs. New York Times Mag. Sept. 27. pp. 92, 97–98, 100, 102.

Berzon, D. R. 1971. *In* R. E. Farber (Comm. of Health, Baltimore, Md.) Weekly Letter to the Mayor. Wk. 48, dated: 3 December.

Berzon, D. R., et al. 1972. Animal bites in a large city—a report on Baltimore, Maryland. Am. J. Pub. Health 62:422–426.

Beskin, C. A., S. H. Colvin, Jr., and P. C. Beaver. 1966. Pulmonary Dirofilariasis: cause of pulmonary nodular disease. J. Am. Med. Assoc. 198:665–667.

Bisseru, B. 1967. Diseases of man acquired from his pets. London: William Heinemann Medical Books. 482 pp.

Bloom, F. 1960. The urine of the dog and cat. New York: Gamma Publications. 84 pp.

Borgaonkar, D. S. et al. 1968. Chromosome study of four breeds of dogs. J. Hered. 59:157–160.

Brobst, D., H. M. Parrish, and F. B. Clack. 1959. The animal bite problem in selected areas of the U. S. Vet. Med. 54:251–256.

Brown, D. H. 1970. Ocular *Toxocara canis*. J. Pediatr. Ophth. 7(3): 182–191.

Burkholder, B. L. :959. Movements and behavior of a wolf pack in Alaska. J. Wildl. Mgt. 23:1–11.

Burt, W. H. 1943. Territoriality and home range concepts as applied to mammals. J. Mamm. 24:346–352.

Caras, R. 1971. Beware of the dog. Family Circle 78(5):18, 20 (May).

Carding, A. H. 1969. The significance and dynamics of stray dog populations with special reference to U. K. and Japan. J. Small Animal Pract. 10(7):419–446.

Census Notes. 1971. A joint release of the Center for Urban Affairs, Johns Hopkins Univ. and Dept. of Planning, Baltimore, Md. Nos. 1–8.

Cohen, A. C. 1960. Estimating the parameters in a conditional Poisson distribution. Biometrics 16:203–211.

Cohen, J. E. 1969. Natural primate troops and a stochastic population model. Am. Naturalist 103:455–477.

———. 1971. Casual groups of monkeys and men. Cambridge, Massachusetts: Harvard University Press. 175 pp.

Cooper, M. 1957. Pica. Springfield, Illinois: Charles C Thomas. 114 pp.

Crawford, K. L. 1964. A survey of animal control activities in Maryland, 1964. Div. Epidemiol. Bureau of Preventive Med. Maryland State Dept. Health. 27 pp.

Crisler, L. 1956. Observations of wolves hunting caribou. J. Mamm. 37:337–346.

Darroch, J. N. 1958. The multiple-recapture census; I. Estimation of a closed population. Biometrika 45:343–359.

Deevey, E. S., Jr. 1947. Life tables for natural populations of animals. Qt. Rev. Biol. 22:283–314.

Dickens, D., and R. N. Ford. 1942. Geophagy (dirt eating) among Mississippi school children. Am. Soc. Rev. 7:59–65.

Dorman, D. W., and J. R. Van Ostrand. 1958. A survey of *Toxocara canis* and *Toxocara cati* prevalence in the New York area. N. Y. State J. Med. September Pt. I:2793–2795.

Dorn, C. R., F. G. Terbrusch, and H. H. Hibbard. 1967. Zoographic and demographic analysis of dog and cat ownership in Alameda Co., Calif., 1965. Berkeley: California Department of Publ. Health. 37 pp.

Ehrenford, F. A. 1957. Canine ascariasis, a source of visceral larva migrans. Am. J. Trop. Med. 6:166–170.

Engle, E. T. 1946. No seasonal breeding cycle in the dog. J. Mamm. 27:79–81.

Faust, E. C., P. C. Beaver, and R. C. Jung. 1968. Animal agents and vectors of human disease. (3rd ed.). Philadelphia: Lea & Febiger. 461 pp.

Fernando, S. T. 1968. Immunological response of the hosts to *Toxocara canis* (Werner, 1782) infection I. Effects of superinfection on naturally infected puppies. Parasitology 58:547–559.

Flanery, J. 1971. Keswick Road residents plan rat protest. Baltimore Morning Sun. 24 July: B18, B5.

Flyger, B. 1970. And man created dog in his own image. Unpublished. 128 pp.

Flyger, V. F. 1959. Comparison of methods for estimating squirrel populations. J. Wildl. Mgt. 23:220–223.

Fox, M. W. 1965. Canine behavior. Springfield, Illinois: Charles C Thomas. 137 pp.

Geyer, J. C., and L. Katz. 1965. Combined sewers, p. 158–167. *In* Restoring the Quality of our Environment: report of the Environmental Pollution Panel, President's Science Advisory Comm. Washington: U. S. Govt. Print. Office.

Glass, D. C., and J. E. Singer. 1971. Behavioral aftereffects of unpredictable and uncontrollable noise. AAAS Symposium: Human Response to Environmental Stimulation. 27 December, Philadelphia.

Goss, L. W., and R. E. Rebrassier. 1922. Demonstration of examination of the feces of the dog for parasitic infestation. N. Am. Vet. 3:177–178.

Hall, J., and B. Sonnenberg. 1956. An apparent case of human infection with the whipworm of dogs, *Trichuris vulpis* (Froelich 1789). J. Parasit. 42:197–199.

Hanson, W. R. 1963. Calculation of productivity, survival, and abundance of selected vertebrates from sex and age ratios. Wildl. Monog. No. 9. 60 pp.

———. 1967. Estimating the density of an animal population. J. Res. Lepidoptera 6:203–247.

————. 1968. Estimating the number of animals: a rapid method for unidentified individuals. Science 162:675–676.

Hawthorne, V. M., et al. 1957. Tuberculosis in man, dog, and cat. Brit. Med. J. 2:675–678.

Hawthorne, V. M., and I. M. Lauder. 1962. Tuberculosis in man, dog, and cat. Am. Rev. Resp. Diseases 85:858–869.

Hayne, D. W. 1949. Calculation of size of home range. J. Mamm. 30: 1–18.

Hebald, Anne. 1969. Wild dogs, man fight to possess dump area. Washington Post. 11 August. p. B1.

Heiner, D. C., and S. V. Kevy. 1956. Visceral larva migrans: report of the syndrome in three siblings. N. Engl. J. Med. 254:629–636.

Herrero, S. 1970. Human injury inflicted by grizzly bears. Science 170: 593–598.

Hirschberg, N., L. Maddry, and M. Hines. 1956. State laboratory confirms leptospirosis in N. Carolina. Public Health Rep. 71:297–298.

Hoag, W. G. 1970. News release on Brucellosis. Mich. State University, Dept. of Information Services, East Lansing. 5 November.

Hogarth-Scott, R. S., S. G. O. Johansson, and H. Bennich. 1969. Antibodies to *Toxocara* in the sera of visceral larva migrans: The significance of raised levels of I_gE. Clin. Exp. Immunol. 5:619–625.

Howard, L. O. 1911. The housefly—a disease carrier. (3rd ed.) New York: Frederick A. Stokes, Co. 312 pp.

Hull, T. G. (Ed.). 1963. Diseases transmitted from animals to man. (5th ed.) Springfield, Illinois: Charles C Thomas. 967 pp.

Huntley, C. C., M. C. Costas, and A. Lyerly. 1965. Visceral lava migrans syndrome: clinical characteristics and immunological studies in 51 patients. Pediatrics 56:523–536.

Hutchinson, G. E. 1971. Killing cockroaches is not enough. AAAS Symposium: Interactions between Natural and Urban Communities. 29 December, Philadelphia.

Iljin, N. A. 1941. Wolf-dog genetics. J. Genetic. 42:359–414.

Jolicoeur, P. 1959. Multivariate geographical variations in the wolf, *Canis lupus* L. Evolution 13:283–299.

Jordan, P. A., P. C. Shelton, and D. L. Allen. 1967. Numbers, turnover, and social structure of the Isle Royale wolf population. Am. Zool. 7:233–252.

Kieran, J. 1959. A natural history of New York City. Boston: Houghton Mifflin Co. 428 pp.

King, J. A. 1954. Closed social groups among domestic dogs. Proc. Am. Phil. Soc. 98:327–336.

Kramer, B. 1971. Awash in excrement, New York fights back against 500,000 dogs. Wall Street Journal. 28 May, p. 1.

Lanphear, F. O. 1970. Vegetation and urban stress: values and problems. AAAS Symposium: Urban Ecology Today. 30 December, Chicago.

Large, T. 1971. The plight—and the threat—of man's best friend. Baltimore Mag., August, pp. 19–21, 56.

Lawrence, B. 1967. Early domestic dog. Sonderdruck aus Z. f. Säugetierkunde Bd. 32 H. 1, S. 44–59.

Leach, M. 1961. God had a dog. New Brunswick, New Jersey: Rutgers University Press. 544 pp.

MacInnes, J. W. 1949. Guard dogs. London: Williams and Norgate, Ltd. 128 pp.

Marx, M. B. and M. L. Furcolow. 1969. What is the dog population? Arch. Environ. Health 19:217–219.

Mattew, W. D. 1930. The phylogeny of dogs. J. Mamm. 11:117–138.

McCarthy, C. 1971. Is Washington really going to the dogs? Washington Post, Potomac Mag. 10 October, pp. 9–10.

McKnight, T. 1961. A survey of feral livestock in California, pp. 28–42. *In* Assoc. of Pacific Coast Geographers Yearbook. Vol. 23. AAAS, Pacific Division.

————. 1964. Feral livestock in Anglo-America. Berkeley: University of California Press. 87 pp.

McMillan, R. B. 1970. Early canid burial from the western ozark highland. Science 167:1246–1247.

McNab, B. K. 1963. Bioenergetics and the determination of home range size. Amer. Naturalist 97:133–140.

Mech, L. D. 1966. The wolves of Isle Royale. U. S. Nat. Park Serv. Fauna Series 7. Washington, D. C.: U. S Govt. Print. Office. 210 pp.

————. 1968. That valuable villain—the wolf. Nat. Wildl. 6(2):2–7.

Milburn, C. L., Jr., and K. E. Ernst. 1953. Eosinophilia-hepatomegaly syndrome of infants and young children; report of a case due to invasion of liver by nematode larvae. Pediatrics 11:358–367.

Murie, A. 1944. The wolves of Mt. McKinley. U. S. Nat. Park Serv., Fauna Ser. 5. Washington: U. S. Govt. Print. Office. 238 pp.

Nobile, P. 1971. Are you really sure dog is man's best friend? Baltimore Evening Sun. 4 October, p. B1.

Overton, W. S. 1971. Estimating the numbers of animals in wildlife populations, pp. 403–456. *In* R. H. Giles, Jr. (ed.). Wildl. Mgt. Techniques (3rd ed.). Washington: Wildlife Society.

Parr, A. E. 1966. Psychological aspects of urbanology. J. Soc. Issues 22(4):39–45.

Parrish, H. M. et al. 1959. Epidemiology of dog bites. Pub. Health Rep. 74:891–903.

Perry, M. C. and R. H. Giles, Jr. 1970. Studies of deer-related dog activity in Virginia. Proc. 24th Ann. Conf. Southeastern Assoc. of Game and Fish Commissioners. pp. 64–73.

Peters, A. H. 1971. Tick-borne Typhus (Rocky Mt. Spotted Fever). J. Am. Med. Assoc. 216:1003–1007.

Phillipson, J. 1966. Ecological energetics. London: Edward Arnold, Ltd. 57 pp.

Pivone, P. P. 1969. What causes the demise of city street trees? New York Times. 21 September. p. 41.

Price, W. H. 1954. The epidemiology of Rocky Mt. spotted fever: Studies on the biological survival mechanism of *Rickettsia rickettsii*. Am. J. Hyg. 60:292–319.

Quarterman, K. D., W. C. Baker, and J. A. Jensen. 1949. The importance of sanitation in municipal fly control. Am. J. Trop. Med. 29:973–982.

Rausch, R. A. 1967. Some aspects of the population ecology of wolves, Alaska. Amer. Zool. 7:253–265.

Reif, J. J., and D. Cohen. 1970. Canine pulmonary diseases and urban environment. II. Retrospective analysis of pulmonary disease in rural and urban dogs. Arch. Environ. Health 20(6):684–689.

Richter, C. P. 1952. Domestication of the Norway rat and its implication for the study of genetics in man. Am. J. Human Genet. 4: 273–285.

Roth, T., M. Kramer, and J. Trinder. 1971. Noise: Sleep, and post-sleep behavior. 3 May, 1971. Sci. Proc. 124th Ann. Meeting Amer. Psychiat. Assoc., Washington.

Rubin, M. L. et al. 1968. An intraretinal nematode. Trans. Am. Acad. Ophth. Otol. 72:855–866.

Shaller, G. B., and G. R. Lowther. 1969. The relevance of carnivore behavior to the study of early hominids. Southwestern J. Anthrop. 25:307–341.

Schiller, E. L. 1967. Progress and problems in the immunodiagnosis of helminthic infection, p. 43–68. *In* H. Sobotka, and C. P. Stewart (ed.). Advan. Clin. Chem. Vol. 9.

Schnabel, Z. E. 1938. The estimation of the total fish population in a lake. Am. Math. Month. 45:348–352.

Schwabe, C. 1969. Veterinary medicine and human health. Baltimore: Williams & Wilkens Co. 713 pp.

Scott, J. P. 1954. The effects of selection and domestication upon the behavior of the dog. J. Nat. Cancer Inst. 15:739–758.

———. 1967. The evolution of social behavior in dogs and wolves. Am. Zool. 7:373–381.

Scott, J. P., and J. L. Fuller. 1965. Genetics and social behavior of the dog. Chicago: University of Chicago Press. 468 pp.

Scott, M. D. 1971. The ecology and ethology of feral dogs in East-Central Alabama. Ph.D. Thesis. Auburn University, Auburn, Alabama. 213 pp.

Siegmund, O. (ed.). 1967. The Merck Veterinary Manual. Merck and Co., Rahway, N. J. 1686 pp.

Sinton, J. 1970. Wildlife in the city: a problem of values. AAAS Symposium: Urban Ecology Today. 30 December in Chicago.

Sloan, W. n.d. Observations of chemical and bacterial quality of Baltimore City storm drain flows. Balt. Harbor Proj. Technical Memo. No. 2 (unpubl.). 6 pp.

Smith, R. L. 1966. Wildlife and forest problems in Appalachia. 31st Nor. Amer. Wildl. Conf. pp. 212–226.

Smythe, N. 1970. The adaptive value of the social organization of the coati (*Nasua narica*). J. Mamm. 51:818–820.

Snyder, C. H. 1961. Visceral larvae migrans: ten years experience. Pediatrics 28:85–91.

Southwick, C. H. 1972. Aggression among non-human primates. Addison-Wesley Modules in Anthropology (in press).

Sprent, J. F. A. 1956. The life history and development of *Toxocara cati* (Shrank 1788), in the domestic cat. Parasitology 46:54–78.

———. 1958. Observations on the development of *Toxocara canis* (Werner 1782) in the dog. Parasitology 48:184–209.

Time. 1970. Do cities really need dogs? Time Mag. 20 July, p. 35.

Time. 1971. The rising wages of fear. Time Mag. 24 May. pp. 80, 82.

Tripp, F. 1971. Parasitic worm blinds boys. Nat. Tattler. 6 June.

Tuazon, R. A., F. Firestone, and A. V. Blaustein. 1967. Human pulmonary Dirofilariasis manifesting as a "coin" lesion. J. Am. Med. Assoc. 199:45–46.

Tysen, F. S. 1968. Nature and urban dweller, pp. 10–18. *In* Man and Nature in the city. U. S. Dept. Interior. Washington: U. S. Govt. Print. Office.

Univ. Denver, Bureau of Business and Soc. Res. 1952. A sample study of some characteristics of the dog population in the city and county of Denver, Summer, 1952. Report to the Dept. of Health and Hospitals, Denver, Colorado. 17 pp.

Vaughn, J., and R. Jordan. 1960. Intestinal nematodes in well-cared-for dogs. Am. J. Trop. Med. Hyg. 9:29–31.

Vermeer, D. E. 1971. Geophagy among the Ewe of Ghana. Ethnology 9:56–72.

Vogl, R. J., and A. M. Beck. 1970. Response of white-tailed deer to a Wisconsin wildfire. Amer. Midl. Naturalist. 84:270–273.

Warren, E. G. 1969. Infection of *Toxocara canis* in dogs fed infected mouse tissues. Parasitology 59:837–841.

Webb, C. H. 1965. Pets, parasites, and pediatrics. Pediatrics 36:521–522.

Webster, G. A. 1956. A preliminary report on the biology of *Toxocara canis* (Werner, 1782). Can. J. Zool. 34:725–726.

Whelton, C. 1971. One kind of crap you don't have to take. New York Village Voice. 25 February.

Wilkinson, C. P., and R. B. Welch. 1971. Intraocular *Toxocara*. Am. J. Ophth. 71:921–930.

Wilder, H. C. 1950. Nematode endophthalmitis. Trans. Am. Acad. Ophth. Otol. 55:99–109.

Wolff, A. H., N. D. Henderson, and G. L. McCallum. 1948. *Salmonella* from dogs and the possible relationship to Salmonellosis in man. Am. J. Pub. Health 38:403–408.

Wool, R. 1971. What about the little fella? Washington Post, Potomac Mag. 10 October. pp. 10–11.

Wright, D. O., and E. M. Gold. 1949. Löfflers syndrome associated with creeping eruption (cutaneous helminthiosis): Report of 26 cases. Arch. Int. Med. 78:303.

Wright, W. H. 1930. The incidence of internal parasites in dogs at Washington, D.C. J. Am. Vet. Med. Assoc. 76:794–803.

Yutuc, L. M. 1949. Prenatal infection of dogs with ascarids, *Toxocara canis* and hookworm, *Ancylostoma canium.* J. Parasit. 35:358–360.

Zinkham, W. H. 1968. Visceral larva migrans due to *Toxocara* as a cause of eosinophilia. Johns Hopkins Med. J. 123:41–47.

Zippen, C. 1958. The removal method of population estimation. J. Wildl. Mgt. 22:82–90.

Index

Composed in Linotype Baskerville by
Monotype Composition Company

Printed offset by Collins Lithographing and Printing
Company on 60 lb. WW&F Mystery Opaque Natural

Bound by Moore and Company in Columbia Bayside Linen BSL 3304